The Soliloquies

ST. AUGUSTINE OF HIPPO

Soliloquies, St. Augustine of Hippo
Jazzybee Verlag Jürgen Beck
86450 Altenmünster, Loschberg 9
Deutschland

Printed by Createspace, North Charleston,
South Carolina, USA

Translated by Rose E. Cleveland (1845 – 1918)

ISBN: 9783849692063

www.jazzybee-verlag.de
www.facebook.com/jazzybeeverlag
admin@jazzybee-verlag.de

CONTENTS:

INTRODUCTION

I

THE anemic society of to-day needs not so much the specializing genius — the artist who lives because of his works — as the all-around man, the vital personality whose works live because of him; the man to whom nothing human is alien, whose experience circumscribes and transcends that of the common lot; the prodigious individual rather than the individual prodigy, the master rather than the marvel. Such an one is Augustine, once Bishop of Hippo, peerless controversialist, incomparable church father; and once, the dreaming, doubting, half-heathen youth and man, eager of brain, restless of heart, lover of pleasure more than lover of God.

M. Nourisson introduces his study of the philosophy of Augustine with the following remark: "If St. Augustine had left only the Confessions and The City of God it would have been easy from them alone to account for the respectful sympathy which environs his memory. How, indeed, can one fail, in The City of God, to admire the flights of genius, and in the Confessions the yet more precious effusions of a great soul? It must be confessed that these portrayals flaming with passion, these ardors of repentance, these wingings toward heavenly things, are what have made the name of the Bishop of Hippo popular. There exists no heart, whatever be its native mediocrity, which is incapable of recognizing something of its own experience in these vacillations, these tempests, these holy transports of Augustine. Hence the prestige conquering centuries, which attaches to this noble figure. However, who does not know him?"

To this question, which implies so widespread an acquaintance with Augustine, one can but reply, Who does know him? How few are they who know even his Confessions, when compared to those who know them not! And still fewer they who know even a small part of the vast City of God.

It is certain, however, that he who knows the Confessions, not to add the City of God, has made acquaintance with Augustine. But the whole man is not there. There is always something, perhaps the main thing, to be learned about a person which the person himself cannot tell. Just as no power can the "giftie gie us," to see ourselves as others see us, so to no one is it given to completely describe himself. The sincerity of his desire to do so can contribute nothing toward the success of his effort. The portrait which the Confessions hang before us is not that of the Soliloquies. The naif convert at Cassiacum had not the self-consciousness which pre-eminence as a church father forced upon the Bishop of Hippo. In the Soliloquies Augustine, — to use the significant slang — completely gives himself away, while in the Confessions he deals himself out in painstaking instalments with conscientious purpose to give full measure, and yet, somehow, comes a little short. This is not to undervalue the incomparable Confessions, but only to note that the impressionist touch in a careless sketch often does more for the likeness than a world of pre-raphaelite detail which may be better art.

Time, also, has something to do with it. The Soliloquies introduce us to the converted man at the very moment of his conversion. The Confessions give us the Bishop of Hippo's recollection of that man after years of absorption in the exacting duties of ecclesiastical function and doctrinal debate. Who, seeking to confront the real self of early years, would accept for such his own random recollections at a much later period, recalled of necessity piecemeal, amid the distractions of professional routine, in exchange for the diary into which was poured at the crucial moment the inmost self of those very days and hours? Harnack says: "The foundations of Augustine's religious characteristics can be best studied in the writings that are read least, namely in the tractates and letters written immediately after his conversion, and forming an extremely necessary supplement to the Confessions." "What was written earlier was, undoubtedly, in many respects less complete, less churchly, more Neoplatonic; but, on the other hand, it was more direct, more personal."

To one who knows how to read them with mental polyglot no work of Augustine gives so much suggestion of his "inexhaustible personality" (Harnack) as do the Soliloquies. But this is true here, as everywhere, only of the prepared reader. The merciless formula, It takes two halves to make a whole one, is never more exacting than in the conjunction of book and reader. He who brings away from a book all which the author puts in it, and all which gets in of itself, is he who takes something to it. It takes a thief to catch a thief. This competent reader will develop con amore the abilities of the comparative anatomist.

In Hippo the writer was shown the bones of a right arm which are piously treasured by believers there as those of Augustine. From these bones a Cuvier could erect the skeleton complete. But the comparative anatomist of psychology can go farther than the physiologist, for from some fragments of his thought carelessly scattered by one who has written, as Augustine tells us he wrote the Soliloquies, after his own heart's cogitation (secundum meum studium et amorem), this psychologist can construct not only the skeleton of the author's personality, but can clothe it with flesh and blood. But this expert is born, not made. That divine thing, sympathy, does it all; for its possessor will not fail to acquire the training needful for its fruitful exercise.

These potential fragments, however, are not found by searching. One stumbles on them. How do we come by our passionate preferences for this poet or that? By a serious setting out to know him in order to find out if we like him? Who ever became a lover of Shakespeare by sitting down before a pile of his complete works to begin at the beginning and solemnly to proceed to the last volume, until every line and word has become familiar? Not one; not one lover at least; for lovers are not formed that way. Rather is he captivated by some stray passage, some scimitar of intuition which pierces to bone and marrow and thrills the reader by its truth and beauty. Transfixed by this wound, more precious than that of Cupid's arrow, he is henceforth Shakespeare's man, with undying passion to hunt, to find, to possess by all means his total treasure. So of Homer, so of Plato, so of Dante, so of Augustine.

II

The Soliloquies of Augustine are almost unknown. This is largely, if not entirely, due to the fact that spurious substitutes have, since the 13th century, usurped their place. Emile Saisset says in his review of Pelissier's translation: "There is, it would seem, scarcely anything among the writings of St. Augustine more familiar to the public, or more widely circulated than the Soliloquies, for the reason that they are not the genuine ones."

It has been the writer's unhappy fortune to experience the truth of M. Saisset's remark. On my library table lies a tiny leathern-bound book, which was black with age and use centuries before its capture from a Milan bookstand by its present owner. The Soliloquies of Augustine had evaded long and persevering search, and to find upon the yellow title-page of this diminutive volume the words: Divi Aurelii Augustini Hippon. Episcopi Meditationes, Soliloquia, etc., etc. — and that, too, in Milan! — was no ordinary satisfaction. It was, therefore, a bitter hour when another discovery was made, to wit, that the title prefacing these Soliloquia covered nothing of Augustine's, save some phrases from the Confessions diluted and adapted to the making of a manual of private devotion. Its editor explains that, "having been repeatedly requested to compose from the monuments of the holy fathers a little book for the stimulation of love and devotion to God, he offers . . . this little collection, etc., etc." The date of the Approbatio, following the Finis, is given as 1607. According to Tillemont this book appeared as early as the 13th century. Poujoulat says it was compiled by Hugo of St. Victor, a monk of the 13th century, from the Confessions and an application of the Rule of St. Augustine made by Hugo himself. It consists of a medley of devout and ejaculatory sentences which could have been produced at any time subsequent to the publication of the Confessions. Erasmus calls it a conglomerate which may be praised rather for its abundance than its importance.

It need not be doubted that this little devotional book, when or by whomsoever compiled, had for its motive, in the first instance, "the stimulation of love and devotion to God." That it should, in many successive editions in the course of seven centuries, retain the name of the Soliloquies of Augustine is a fact not so amiably accepted. One may believe that its first editor might have been ignorant of the existence of the genuine Soliloquies. It is true that the Saxon king, Alfred, translated them into the English of his day in the 10th century, a fact that would suggest that they could not be wholly unknown to Latins of the same or later days. Still, acquaintance with sources would be most likely confined to ecclesiastical authorities, and it is quite credible that such in those days, as in ours, would deem a "collection" of pious ejaculations of a sound Catholic type much safer reading for the masses than the intensely thoughtful and speculative pages of an author not yet purged of Neoplatonic and Manichaean taints. Such speculation bearing the name of the incomparable church father, the defender par excellence of the faith, the canonized saint, written, too, after his conversion, would be unspeakably embarrassing to father-confessors. Reflections such as these would lead, by easy logic, to a suggestion irresistible to the zealous monk. Why not a little book bearing the name Soliloquies compiled from the Confessions and other works consistent with the church father, which would dispose of the whole difficulty, retire the "offspring" (Soliloquies I, 1) and put the edifying bastard in its place? This pious plan would have been quite safe of execution in those days; possibly not so much so in these when libraries exist, accessible to all, where the complete works of Augustine may be found in the original text, the precious fragment bearing the name of Soliloquies, among them. Alfred of England is known better to-day than he was a thousand years ago, and the Saissets, Janets,

Pelissiers, Labothonières and hosts of comrades in swelling ranks of those who are awaking or are already wide-awake to the *immenza grandezza* (Il Santo Fogazzaro) of Augustine the man, will not permit him longer to remain submerged in the church father. The genuine Soliloquies, with other of his earlier works, will win their rightful place in the representation of that "inexhaustible personality," whom Harnack also calls the first modern man.

The spurious Soliloquies are, however, still being published under Augustine's name. A late edition (1891, Victor Lecoffre, Paris) is announced by the editor as a "new translation revised very accurately after the Latin," continuing: "It is true that, although these appear under the name of the incomparable Doctor, many hold that it is uncertain whether they are his. . . . One may however rest assured that, if they are not the saint's as to arrangement, they are altogether his as to matter." Here, again, is no suggestion of the existence of the genuine Soliloquies, and one may take his choice between two explanatory theories, the one that each successive republisher of this book is always ignorant that genuine Soliloquies exist; the other that in his great zeal against the spirit of modernism with which they are replete, he is constrained, by loyalty to the good cause, to repeat the silence of his predecessors concerning them. However this may be, it is evident that Augustine's genuine Soliloquies have not, in the past, been considered important to the church, or to himself in the rôle of church father. Nor can it be affirmed that they will be so considered in the future. Though, in the true sense of the word, they are theological, discoursing of God, "the one Reality," they are not dogmatic or ecclesiastical. No "system" can be founded, or even suggested by them, no institutional Christianity. They contain much in suggestion and in spirit of that abomination of desolation to the Vatican Catholic, modernism, but nothing of that ecclesiastical technique which has fitly joined together and floated over all waters these many centuries the massive ark of St. Peter's. They supply no hint of the career ahead for their author, none of the bishop to be, the prince of controversialists, the defender of the faith, none of the canonized saint.

On the other hand there is more than hint, there is ample revelation of all that went to the making of the man of two worlds, the man to whom nothing of man is alien; whose intellect absorbs all knowledge as his heart all experience, fusing the two, and forcing the resultant through the meshes of his keen dialectic, whence it emerges sifted for the service of God and man. In this fragmentary monologue is found a superlative example of the unceasing action of this combination of his thought and feeling as it moves, like a radius, within that infinite circle where God is centre in the soul of man and circumference in the infinitude of being.

It is not within the proprieties of this preface to discuss the rank or reach of Augustine's intellect, or to argue for or against Harnack, when he says he is the first modern man and credits him with "a wealth of psychological discoveries," "as regards memory, association of ideas, synthetic activity of spontaneous thought, ideality of the categories, a priori functions, determinant numbers, synthesis of reproduction in the imagination," etc. (History of Dogma, p. 112, and note); or to bring forward the multitude of great names from his own day to this, who testify to his superlative endowments; but only to let him speak to heart and brain alike of the reader, in the unself-conscious sample which is here presented.

The interest of this remarkable fragment to most readers, aside from its religious importance, is mainly psychological and historical. It has also other distinct and inestimable values, which cannot be even touched upon here. To the student of Neoplatonism and other related philosophies it is a mine of suggestion. (Among countless others an important recent appreciation of this value is M. Grandgeorge's St. Augustin et La Neoplatonisme, Ernest Leroux, Paris.) It contains valuable samples of the harassing dialectics in which, after Socrates and Plato, he was trained, and in which the pupil excelled the master. It contains what Pelissier calls an excellent moral argument for the immortality of the soul. Spite of the jealousy of the worshipers of Descartes, it originates in the dialogue between Reason and Augustine which introduces the second book, — elaborated elsewhere, especially in the City of God (see note 53) — the famous cogito ergo sum which is the corner-stone of modern Cartesian philosophy. His analysis of the will supplies a primer of first principles to modern psychology (see note 12). Augustine taught, before Kant immortalized the truth in his Critique, "The only good thing is the good will." But when all is said, the main artery which connects Augustine so vitally with every one who knows him, is that current of passionate love for God and the soul, so conspicuous in the Soliloquies, which makes him kin — if king — of the whole race by the reddest blood of the human heart.

"The fourteen centuries fall away
Between us and the Afric saint,
And at his side we urge to-day
The immemorial quest and old complaint."

The great man is the great lover; the greatest he whose greatest love is for the greatest. Always a lover, loving life, love, man, woman, letters, discourse, with inexhaustible passion, Augustine coasted half his life at his peril among the rocks and over the shallows along the shore of the vast deep which waited for him far beyond. But now at thirty-three years of age when we meet him in the Soliloquies, he has gone to sea with God. Flood-tide has lifted him off the perilous ledges of his passions, and, fearless in those unsounded depths where pilot and port are one (Soliloquies I, 4), all the currents of his soul set to one course, — "God and the soul," "the soul and God alone!" At this solemn interval moment we see him in communion with the immanent Deity concerning the issues of life. Behind him lies his past in ruins; before him looms his future in nebulae; between these Augustine questions and prays: "Teach me how to come to Thee! I have nothing but the will. I know nothing but that the fleeting and failing should be spurned, the certain and eternal sought. This I do, Father, for this is all I know: but how to make my way to Thee I know not. Do Thou suggest it, make it plain, equip me for the journey! If they who take refuge in Thee, find Thee by faith, give me faith! If by virtue, give me virtue! If by knowledge, give me knowledge!"

III

The first page of the Soliloquies brings us face to face with those two Augustines which are to be met with henceforth in all his works, the one practical, the other speculative; the one seeking for himself, — as in the Soliloquies, — or for others, — as in his later official works, — principles for the regulation of conduct; the other seeking everywhere, with consummate psychology, a pathway to ultimate reality. Already in the Soliloquies he recognizes with anguish the world-wide difference between believing and knowing, "for it may be truly said that we believe all that we know, but not that we know all that we believe" (I, 3).

At this moment he is seeking both what to do and how to know. His former point of view as to the desirable things of life has entirely passed away. With his newness of will all things have become new, and he begins his Soliloquies by relating how, for a long time and with intense anxiety, he has been turning over in his mind a multitude of alternatives, seeking to know his true self, and what, as his best good, he should seek, what, as an evil, he should shun; and that, while thus revolving in his mind this incessant query, he is aware of a sudden interposition in the debate of "one" of whom he is vividly conscious, yet, he adds in parenthesis, though it be the one thing of all others he most eagerly strives to learn, he does not know whether this "one" is himself or another, and, if another, whether that other be within or without himself. In present-day language of psychology, he is asking whether he shall recognize this "other" as a subliminal self, or a secondary personality, or an extra Augustine immanent in the Cosmic Absolute, or as part and parcel of the All-Becoming-ness whose bright ray of less impeded self-hood constitutes the real Augustine? Or, by a sharp turn, will an inveterate dualism assert itself — Athanasius contra mundum — and explain that one and one — or this and the "other" — make two? Theories these, which in varying formulae have traveled down the ages, only stopping anywhere long enough to change their clothes and get themselves different names. Theosophies, monisms, dualisms, pluralisms, they arrive from a far past to be the guests in modern dress of modern hosts, and as such to be hailed by most as modern discoveries. But they were old acquaintances, with ancient names, to Augustine. In his Retractations, written late in life, Augustine tell us that in his Soliloquies he questions and answers himself as if two, reason and himself, were discussing, although he was quite alone (me interrogans, me respondens, tanquam duo essemus, ratio et ego, cum solus essem). He gives Reason the place of preceptor, Augustine taking the place of pupil. Reason forthwith, having briefly led his pupil to a realization of the practical difficulties in the way of his undertaking, exhorts him to "at once pray for health and help."

In this initial behest of Reason is seen that involution of reason and faith which is the most constant characteristic of Augustine's thought. Reason speaks for and to the reasonable. It is no discouraged tyro who, beset with embarrassment as to ways and means by which to pursue his longed-for research, turns in desperation from intellect to faith. It is that most competent and authoritative entity, Reason, which anticipates the failure incident upon any other course than that of optimistic co-operation, through the appeal of faith, with the source of reason and knowledge. Already it is clear to the practical Augustine that rationabiliter visum est, ut fides praecedit intellectum. It is never a matter of trying God, when other experiments have failed. God lacks neither power nor willingness; it is only a question of our ability to desire the best thing, and to get ready to receive it. At the commencement of the second book, Augustine rises to Reason's height and counsels the exercise of faith first of all — "Let us believe that God will be with us!" To which Reason replies, implying that hitherto faith has not been perfect, "Let us actually believe this if it be within our power!" In reply to which Augustine, summing up in the words his whole "system," replies: "He is our power!"

For Augustine all symbols of safety and fruition are epitomized in that one word, God, the only Reality. Whatever his traditions, or his speculations, he is, on his religious side, a practical monist. God is all: and nowhere is this sublime spiritual monism so formulated as in this prayer, which, in response to Reason's exhortation, introduces the Soliloquies. Everywhere Augustine proclaims this as postulate: it is unthinkable that man should feel sufficient to himself. Not only in his Confessions when he talks to God, as father-confessor, but in all his works after conversion, is seen this habitual consciousness of God, as the one Reality. "God, true and perfect Life, in whom and by whom and through whom those live who do truly and perfectly live!" And this consciousness deepened and broadened like the stream which descends from the hills and invades one field after another until the whole plain is overflowed. So as time goes on the Divine flood is to fill his landscape and to obliterate all other things. At present, in the Soliloquies, we see this flood descending, in spite of the habit of the Platonist, the Neoplatonist, the Manichaean. "The vanity of the schools" of which in his Retractations he accuses the Soliloquies, has, as yet, left its high places, which the deeps of God have not completely hidden. Augustine, the dialectician emerges; but if so, is he more harmful or more intrusive here, than as the controversialist of a later day? If the latter was a power for the church, of his day, is not the former a power for a purer devotion, a more single zeal — "love for God and the soul alone" — for all time and all believers?

As a Neoplatonist, not less than as a Christian, Augustine knows that Reason, whatever be its substance, plays between himself and God. "Ratio was, to him, the organ in which God reveals himself to man, and in which man perceives God" (History of Dogma, V, p. 125, n).

If the Soliloquies have any dogmatic value, that is, if they supply the thinker with any constructive material, it is to be found here in the first formulation of that which was the corner-stone of all his practical as well as doctrinal teaching: Fides praecedit intellectum. Everywhere, this precious ore gleams constant amid all his conglomerates, separate, yet involved in the whole structure; implied in its very form of dialogue between the ego, and the ego-plus. Reason shadows forth a teaching concerning faith which is reason, and concerning reason which is faith: the separation is only in function. Intuition precedes knowledge, is knowledge by another route; "that direct self-consciousness of the spirit in regard to itself which sleeps in every mind, but which few remark and still fewer interpret" (Naturalism and Religion, Otto). It is the believing before seeing; "Kant's rational faith whose belief is grounded in the categorical imperative" (the thing that ought to be true and therefore is true; the mandates of Duty) "and guaranteed by it" (Philosophy of the Christian Religion, Fairbairn). This knowing which is intuition, insight; this believing which is faith, foresight, is the intellectus in its purity of germ; the dogma without the formula. Intuition and faith do not talk; they see.

Perhaps to many the Soliloquies supply no such constructive suggestion: to him who says they have none no argument need be made. But where the hammer hits the red-hot metal the sparks will fly. Better be still and catch, if only one of these divine scintillations, holding it close against the heart that no wind of words may quench its sacred fire. Tended carefully, a flame will mount to the brain where intellectus waits to perform his alchemy.

Shall we now, as in duty bound, interject some mention of the obvious defects of the Soliloquies? They are on the surface and need no emphasizing. Pelissier in the notes to his fine translation of the Soliloquies, says: "We suffer to see a doctrine so pure and true compromised by its mixture with these miserable sophisms." And in his Introduction we read: "In the Soliloquies, last adieu of a pious soul to philosophical controversies, one can admire, with a sort of secret preference, an ardor of youth which time, in disciplining, must enfeeble. Under the rhetorician who takes delight in submerging beneath the billows of scholastic arguities an excellent moral argument, one feels the young Christian who seeks and senses in advance the solution of his problem. . . . Thus, in the birth-brightness of the Christian genius, the stains and imperfections of detail are effaced and lost in order that we may abandon ourselves wholly to the fruitful and generous enjoyment of admiration."

Comparing small things to great, we may say of the Soliloquies what Dr. Marcus Dodd says, in the Introduction to his translation of the stupendous City of God: "Though there are in it, as in all ancient books, things that seem to us childish and barren, there are also the most surprising anticipations of modern speculations. . . . It is true there are passages which can possess an interest only to the antiquarian; there are others with nothing to redeem them but the glow of their eloquence; there are many repetitions; there is an occasional use of arguments 'plus ingenieux que solides' as M. Saisset says. . . . The book has its faults; but it effectually introduces us to the most influential of theologians and the greatest popular teacher; to a genius that cannot nod for many lines together; to a reasoner whose dialectic is more formidable . . . than that of Socrates or Aquinas; to a saint whose ardent and genuine devotional feeling bursts up through the severest argumentation; to a man whose kindliness and wit, universal sympathies and breadth of intelligence lend piquancy and vitality to the most abstract dissertation."

And now for a glance at Augustine as he soliloquizes, and then we will leave him to the reader.

IV

The book which a great genius writes con amore is the book one cares to read, for whatever be its defects, it has this pre-eminent merit: that, more than another can, it reveals the author himself. We have seen that Augustine wrote the Soliloquies to please himself. We shall now see that he wrote them in an environment pleasing to him, for he had with him those friends whom he so desires shall with him, "inquire into God and the soul" (I, 20); and he enjoys ease and comfort in the beautiful retirement he craves. The little village of Casciago, nested among the mountains surrounding Milan and the Italian lakes, wears to-day the same bewitching features of natural scenery which so charmed Augustine in the year 386. The tourist who goes there gazes with enchantment on the same superb panorama. Throned on the northwest Monte Rosa in perpetual ermine queens it over her Alpine courtiers grouped about in close attendance, while lower heights stand knightly guard, and between their steadfast columns the waters of Maggiore and the lesser lakes put in gleams as of their knightly steel. To the south stretches the great plain of Lombardy with its fertile fields, its hamlets and its villages, all humbly tributary to the royal city farther on.

But no tourist goes to Casciago to-day unless he goes there for Augustine's sake — to stand, for a moment, where Augustine "rested in God from the fiery turmoil of the world." His Confessions tell us of this fiery turmoil. For him, as for every one not wholly of it, the world had been no resting place. Augustine had always been of two worlds and therefore never at home in either. The thirty-three years behind him had been lived under a succession of conflicting influences into which he was born. His birthplace, Thagaste, a small inland town in North Africa now Soul Aras, was partly of the old, partly of the new religion. His mother was a Christian, his father a pagan, though converted to his wife's faith before his death. The history of his boyhood and youth is a record of excessive antagonisms and excessive predilections, of passionate joys and passionate sorrows such as a nature at once fiery and tender must experience amid the "contrary currents of the world." Reaching a young manhood of splendid ability he soon makes for himself a distinguished name in his profession of rhetoric, which was then almost comprehensive in its scope, embracing philosophy and literature as well as disputation and oratory. But now, as earlier, hot blood and a hungry heart battle with a lofty spirit and sensitive conscience, and the weary warfare of flesh against spirit and spirit against flesh does not cease until he wrenches loose from it in its crisis agony in the lonely garden at Milan. The passion for truth, for knowledge, for debate, that "chain of reasoning" which he says (Epistles, III) "I am accustomed to caress as if it were my chief treasure, and in which I take, perhaps, too much delight" was too often and too long subjected to the "very toy of toys and vanity of vanities," his antiquae amiciae (Confessions, VIII, p. 201), the ministers to the lust of the flesh, the lust of the eyes, the pride of life. "I was sick and tormented, tossing and turning me in my chains;" alternating between the "two wills" which he found a horrifying monster (monstrum horrendum). We see him at Carthage, at Rome, at Milan, studying, teaching, lecturing; making joyous, generous friendships, flattered and championed by powerful friends, maintaining faithfully for years one woman, with his son and mother; yielding to the solicitations of his mother and friends in their plans for an advantageous marriage, which should have put an end to this irregular connection, and advance him in emolument and honor and all that goes with successful and reputable citizenship; but ever and always the hunger of the heart for love, the fire of the brain for knowledge, consume him with "a fever of irresolution." "The very moment in which I was to become another man, the nearer it approached me, the greater horror did it strike into me; but it did not strike me back nor turn me aside, but kept me in suspense" (Confessions, IX). Already entering middle life, these struggles had drained the youth from him but left its tyrannous desires and habits. Many years had passed since the Hortensius of Cicero had, at nineteen, changed his ideals and aspirations "to an incredible ardor for an immortality of wisdom." And now, in the words of Paul Janet in the introduction to his superb translation of the Confessions which must not suffer by translation: "Que nous voilà loin de ce premier éveil de l'âme, de cet appel à la sagesse, de cet aurore de la pensée, où tout est beau et facile, où les passions sont un auxiliare plutôt qu'un obstacle! La pensée s'est fatiguée; l'affirmation, si facile à la jeunesse, est devenue un effort pénible; les déceptions ont enfanté le dégoût; le désir du repos, du bonheur facile, des honneurs mondains, commence à gagner sur l'amour du beau et du bien. L'âme n'a pas renoncé encore à son beau rêve, mais elle se sent fléchir; état périlleux, où beaucoup d'âmes et de volontés succombent, mais d'où une âme forte et grande sort éprouvée, retrempée, et prête aux plus grands sacrifices. C'est ce qui arriva à Saint Augustin." The crisis of conflict between the two wills, the one old, the other new, the one carnal, the other spiritual, is now reached; the great surrender succeeds to this climax agony, and the fig-tree in the garden of his lodging at Milan shelters now the new man! "And this was the result, that I willed not to do what I willed, and willed to do what Thou willed'st. . . . How sweet did it suddenly become to me to be without trifles! And what, at one time, I feared to lose, it was now a joy to me to put away. For Thou did'st cast them away from me, Thou true and highest sweetness. Thou did'st cast them away, and, instead of them, did'st enter in Thyself, sweeter than all pleasures, though not to flesh and blood, brighter than all light but more veiled than all mysteries; more exalted than all honor but not to the exalted in their own conceits. Now was my soul free from the gnawing cares of seeking and getting and of wallowing and exciting the itch of lust, and I babbled unto Thee, my brightness, my riches and my health, the Lord, my God!" (Confessions, IX).

With this new mind there can be, for Augustine, no thought of the old life. All is changed; there is but one next thing. "And it seemed good to me as before Thee, not tumultuously to snatch away, but gently to withdraw the service of my tongue from the talker's trade . . . and, being redeemed by Thee, no more to return for sale." Still the "hot-blooded man," (Harnack) he is now possessed by his last all-dominating passion, the love of God and the soul, and in its high rapture he turns his back forever upon the world with its fever and fret, not, however, without occasional intrusion of his faint following "Shadows" as the reader of the Soliloquies will see.

Augustine took with him to the villa of his friend at Casciago a little company of those much loving and much beloved, tried and tested by long companionship, of one mind as to intellectual things, of one purse as to material things; not, as yet, all of them Christians, but all alike absorbed in the pursuit of knowledge, and the love of philosophical discourse. Of this company were Augustine's mother, Monica, whom all the world knows, she whom Augustine describes as "with the woman's garb but a man's faith, cleaving to us in the tranquillity of age in motherly love and Christian piety"; Alypius, Augustine's townsman, fellow and follower from lecture-room to episcopal chair, himself being a bishop in Thagaste when Augustine was Bishop of Hippo; Adeodatus, Augustine's son by the woman greatly loved and mourned, to whom he was faithful until she parted from him, in anticipation of his marriage (Confessions, VI, 15). Of this youth he says: "His talents inspired me with awe. . . . Though scarcely fifteen years of age, he surpassed in talent many learned and venerable men. . . . There is a book of his and mine entitled Concerning the Master; . . . the sentiments put into the mouth of my fellow in that dialogue are all his own." Added to these there were Evodius, formerly an officer of the court of the Emperor, one of the agentes in rebus, who after his conversion and baptism resigned from the royal service in order that "he might the better prepare himself for the service of God" (Confessions, IX, 8). A brother, two cousins, and two pupils completed the community. One of these pupils was the gay and gifted Licentius, son of Augustine's wealthy and powerful friend, Romanianus, to whom he was indebted for much material aid in his professional career, and to whom he rendered overflowing intellectual and spiritual returns, as is seen by many references to him, expecially in the first book written at Casciago, Contra Academicos. That the son shared his father's enthusiasm for Augustine appears evident in a paragraph from one of his letters to his master, quoted in Augustine's reply (Epistles, XXVI). This extract seems to be from a sort of poem inspired by recollections of Casciago written to Augustine and reads thus: "Oh that the morning light of other days could, with its gladdening chariot, bring back to me bright hours which are gone, hours spent together in the heart of Italy among its high mountains, when proving the generous leisure and pure privilege which belong to the good! Neither stern winter with its frozen snow, nor the rude blasts of Zephyrus and raging of Boreas could deter me from following your footsteps with eager tread. You have only to express your wish." Lanciani asserts that the tomb of Licentius was discovered in the church of San Lorenzo at Rome, bearing insignia and inscriptions showing that he had attained the rank of Roman senator and had died a Christian.

Other friends, equally congenial, but unable to join the little company in person, were corresponding members. The lovely and beloved Nebridius, whose letters to and from Augustine reveal each in characteristic quality, are inestimable souvenirs of the days and nights which gave birth to the Soliloquies. The generous Verecundus also, who, though prevented by his marriage from becoming a member of the community, placed his villa at Casciago at its disposal. Of this friend, and his generous service, Augustine says after his death (Confessions, IX, 3): "For that country-place of his where we rested in Thee from the fiery turmoil of the world, Thou dost now repay Verecundus with the freshness of Thy evergreen Paradise, for in that mountain of curds, Thy mountain, that fruitful mountain, Thou hast loosed him from the sins of earth" (translator's version). The poet Zenobius is also invoked, though at this moment, Augustine tells us (Book II), "far away in transalpine leisure composing a poem by which the fear of death is driven away, and that chill and stupor of the soul, unyielding as the ice of ages, is cast out." These and others of congenial tastes are in sympathetic rapport and doubtless hear of the thought and speech of the residents who, gathered daily and hourly round the master, abandon themselves to the full enjoyment of the half-year's opportunity — from Autumn's vintage to Easter.

The symposium has full play along Platonic and Neoplatonic as well as Pauline lines. The stenographer is ever-present and dialogues and debates are committed to his waxen tablet as, one after another, they fall from the lips of the master and those of his associates. The Soliloquies alone are written down by Augustine himself as "they cannot be dictated, since they demand absolute solitude (Book I, 1)."

In these various books, written at Casciago and in the Confessions, Augustine gives us many glimpses of his life there. Meditation and prayer occupy many hours of the night and early morning, and prepare him for the intellectual exercise of the day, which, for the most part, takes the form of debate and dialogue. The magnetism of his personality and the interest of the theme discussed rivet the attention of each of his audience upon the master, whose native tact as well as great skill acquired in the long practice of conducting the rhetorical education of others, win from all a ready response to questions put by him.

The 13th of November it is remembered that Augustine's thirty-third birthday has arrived, and it is celebrated by the initiation, after a simple dinner with his friends, of a discussion which lasts three days, and results in the book entitled The Happy Life. Here is a sample page (see Tableau de l'Éloquence Chrétienne au IVe Siècle, Villemain).

" 'Is the man happy, who obtains that which he desires?' I asked. My mother thereupon replied: 'If he desires what is good and obtains it, he is happy. But if he wishes for that which is evil, even if he obtain it, he is wretched.'

" 'My mother,' said I, smiling my approval, 'you have attained the summit of philosophy. Though you lack the language in which he elaborates it, you have expressed the thought of Cicero in his Hortentius, a book which he wrote in the praise and for the defence of philosophy. He says there exist men, not indeed philosophers, yet skilled in debate, who declare that those are happy who devote their lives to obtaining pleasure: but that this is an error. For to desire that which is unseemly is, itself, the worst of evils. One is less miserable in failing to attain, than in desiring to attain that which is bad; the corruption of the will bringing in its defeat less of ill than its gratification could of happiness.' "

"At these words of mine an exclamation escaped my mother, such as would have been fitting had a great personage been the speaker: but I well knew in what Divine source these verities had their origin."

Augustine's companions agree that happiness consists in the possession of God, since obedience to His will and right conduct follow. Thereupon Augustine continues:

" 'This inner admonition which compels us to the thought of God, to the thirst for Him, to the search after Him, comes to us from the source of all truth. It is the sun which shines within our souls. It is the truth which we divine when, our eyes being too feeble, or too suddenly opened, we are afraid to look it in the face. It is none other than God, Himself, in His changeless perfection. So long as we persist in seeking to satisfy our thirst elsewhere than at this fountain, we must admit that we have not attained our proper goal, and therefore, though God be for us, we are neither wise nor happy. Complete satisfaction of souls, the truly happy life, is to know purely and fully what Truth itself is, what conducts in the search after it, and by what relations it connects us with the supreme perfection. These three demonstrate to purified souls the one only God, the one only Reality, in distinction from the self-contradicting fables of superstition.'

"Here my mother, reminded of words graven on her memory, as if startled from a dream by the familiar accents of her faith, recited with transport the words of the priest: 'Holy Trinity receive our prayer!' and added: 'Yes, this is the happy life, to which one should expect to be swiftly conducted by steadfast faith, by lively hope, by burning charity!' "

In the Confessions (IX, 4) Augustine gives us a glimpse of his communings in solitude at Casciago:

"What utterances sent I up unto Thee, my God, when I read the psalms of David, those faithful songs and sounds of devotion which excludes all swelling of spirit, when, new to Thy true love, at rest in the villa with Alypius, a catechumen like myself, my mother cleaving unto us, in woman's garb truly but with a man's faith, with the peacefulness of age, full of motherly love and Christian piety! What utterances used I to send up unto Thee in those Psalms, and how was I inflamed towards Thee by them, and burned to rehearse them, if it were possible, throughout the whole world, against the pride of the human race! With what vehement and bitter sorrow was I indignant at the Manichaeans! . . . I wished that they had been somewhere near me then, and, without my being aware of their presence, could have beheld my face, and heard my words, when I read the fourth psalm in that time of my leisure — how that psalm wrought upon me! — oh, that they might have heard what I uttered on these words without my knowing whether they heard or no, lest they should think I spake it because of them! For of a truth neither should I have said the same things, nor in the way I said them, if I had perceived that I was heard and seen by them: and had I spoken them, they would not so have received them as when I spake by and for myself before Thee, out of the private feelings of my soul. I alternately quaked with fear and warmed with hope and with rejoicing in Thy mercy, oh Father!

"I read further — 'Be ye angry and sin not.' And how was I moved oh, my God, who had now learned to 'be angry' with myself for the things past, so that in the future I might not sin! . . . Nor were my 'good things' now without, nor were they sought after with the eyes of flesh in that sun; for they that would have joy from without easily sink into oblivion, and are wasted upon those things which are seen and temporal, and in their starving thoughts do lick their very shadows. Oh, if only they were wearied out with their fasting, and said, 'Who will show us any good?' . . . Oh that they could behold the internal Eternal, which, having tasted, I gnashed my teeth that I could not show It to them! . . . But there, where I was angry with myself in my chamber, when I was inwardly pricked, where I had offered my 'sacrifice,' slaying my old man and beginning the resolution of a new life — there had'st Thou began to grow sweet unto me, and to 'put gladness in my heart.' And I cried out as I read this outwardly and felt it inwardly. Nor would I be increased with worldly goods, wasting my time and being wasted by time; whereas I possessed in Thy eternal simplicity other corn and wine and oil."

One would have almost consented to pose as a Manichaean for the time, if by such a pious fraud a glance at this Augustine could have been had. Oh, that the notarius of those days had carried along with his stylus the camera which accompanies his successor of to-day!

Painters, from Botticelli to Ary Scheffer, and before and since, have, each after his own heart, conceived the features of "the Afric saint." The only conception, however, which the writer has seen, which approaches adequacy in its suggestions, is that of Botticelli, whose soft fresco on a column, in the church of All Saints in Florence, was, according to Vasari, considered a masterpiece in the painter's day. It represents Augustine at a period of life much later than that of the Soliloquies, and is scarcely the Augustine we think of at Casciago.

According to Poujoulat, the most painstaking research has failed to determine which among all the tribes of the North Africa of Augustine's day, is that from which he sprung. The Kabyles of to-day are believed to be the descendants of one of these tribes — the ancient Getulians, of whom Sallust speaks as a race of men, both uncultured and unconquered (genus hominum ferum et incultumque). At Algiers one hears it said that the Kabyles, who live on the hills north of the city, having no community with the rest of the world, have never been conquered. From the days of the first Roman invasion and conquest of the Mediterranean coast, they have retired farther and farther inland, and higher and higher upland, yielding their territory but never themselves to the tide of conquest. One is impressed with their nobility of feature and dignity of bearing as they pass, haughty and detached, along the streets of Algiers, in a day's descent from their heights on affairs of business, never, one is sure, of pleasure. The type is marked with character and intellect, and it is not difficult to persuade one's self that in it is much of that which Botticelli saw when he put his masterpiece on the column of All Saints. If a composite could be struck from this glorious fresco, and the glorious face of a Kabyle boy, which is to be seen in many photograph shops of Algiers, one might fancy be could gain from it a conception of the aspect of the Augustine who discoursed with his friends at Casciago on the folly of the wise Academicians, on the cosmic Order of God's universe, on the truly Happy Life, and, last of all, with himself alone on God and the Soul and the problem of its immortality. At thirty-three the rounded contours of the young Kabyle would have been lost in the lines of passion and pain traced by the intense life of heart and mind upon the famous rhetorician's face, though not yet deepened into those furrows ploughed deep by the cure of souls and the care of the churches, which Botticelli puts into the face of the bishop still in his prime. One needs but to turn some pages in the Confessions, those especially in which the story of the long and fierce struggle ending in that "complete conversion" for which he still prays in that wonderful prayer which introduces the Soliloquies, to realize the warrant Botticelli had for putting into his great fresco that intensity of thought and feeling which startles the beholder. One is almost satisfied with the conception for he feels himself to be gazing into the soul, rather than upon the face, of a lion of intellect and feeling, — a kingly Numidian lion tamed by truth and love to fathomless deeps of compassion and sympathy, and boundless powers of service; nay, rather into the soul of the greatest of God's warriors, where the battle has, indeed, left piteous scars, but where victory has planted its peace!

V

In many of the principal cities of the world there are now libraries where the complete works of Augustine can be found, and among them, occupying a very few pages in the first of the many huge volumes, the Soliloquies. The original text has not, to the writer's knowledge, been published in separate form, although a German house has lately issued it with others, perhaps all, of his works, in convenient volumes for those who desire to possess them. It was more satisfactory to me to transcribe it from the huge Benedictine volume by hand. After this tedious task was completed, M. Pelissier's fine translation into French (1853), containing the Latin text, was, with much difficulty, procured in Paris. The book was said to be out of print and only the most painstaking perseverance of a friend succeeded in obtaining for me this portable copy. The vicious virtue of expurgation has touched Pelissier's translation, for which however he is not, presumably, responsible, as the text from which he translates and which accompanies his translation is without the expurgated passages. No mention is made of the edition used by him, and it is perhaps less inconceivable that Pelissier himself caused their expurgation from the text he supplies, than that any reprint of an authentic Benedictine edition should have been so mutilated. The present version has omitted nothing found in the Benedictine text. So far as can be learned, but two English translations of Augustine's Soliloquies have been published previous to the present venture. The first of these is attributed to King Alfred of England in the tenth century. This version was done into twentieth century English by Henry Lee Hargrove, professor of English in Baylor University, Waco, Texas, in 1904, and is to be found as Number XXII in the series of Yale Studies in English. The text is only partially followed by Alfred, Mr. Hargrove estimating that he rejected about three-fourths of the Latin of Augustine, so that, what with his naïve rejections, and equally naïve interjections, this version, charming and valuable as it is, can for obvious reasons only by excess of mendacious courtesy be called a translation of Augustine's Soliloquies, being far less representative of Augustine than of Alfred. The value, however, of Mr. Hargrove's beautiful work cannot be over-estimated. That it cannot make its readers acquainted with the Soliloquies of Augustine is scarcely a loss, since it is sure to beget a desire for such acquaintance which can be easily gratified by the reader of simple Latin, and it does add immensely to one's acquaintance with Alfred. Mr. Hargrove's first object was not to widen the circle of Augustine's admirers, but to exploit the English of Alfred's day, which he does — and incidentally Alfred himself as a matter of course — in his preceding pamphlet King Alfred; Old English Version of St. Augustine's Soliloquies (1902). It is easy to see, however, that Mr. Hargrove fell in love with the Augustine of the Soliloquies, as in the case of many another affaire du cœur, by happy accident, and by his following (1904) version of his previous version into modern English, has done much for other lovers of both Augustine and Alfred.

The other, more properly called a translation, referred to may be found in Vol. VII of the Select Library of the Nicene and post-Nicene Fathers, edited by the late Dr. Philip Schaff. This was done by the Rev. Charles Starbuck, and to be appreciated, both in its excellencies and defects, should be compared with the original, which does not accompany it. The brief preface of less than a page should also be read in the light of the historical facts.

For the translation here presented nothing is claimed save that which a persistent effort to render the author's thought into clear everyday English may merit. In this connection it should be said that all citations from Augustine's other works, when not elsewhere credited, are taken from translations to be found in the St. Augustine Series published by T. & T. Clark, Edinburgh.

This book has no other raison d'être than the translator's intense desire that Augustine the man, apart from the ecclesiastic, shall be better known. The reader who sympathizes with this motive will need no other appeal for charity in considering its many shortcomings. Even the length and occasional apparent irrelevance of the notes will be indulged if help toward the desired end is thus obtained. Augustine's paramount value does not lie in the fact that "he was the most astonishing man in the Latin Church" (Villemain, Tableau de l'Éloquence Chrétienne au IVe Siècle) but rather in the solace and significance of his "inexhaustible personality" to every soul who, with him, has come to realize that "the fleeting and the failing should be spurned, the steadfast and eternal sought." That such readers will obtain from these Soliloquies enlarged acquaintance with their author is the hope of the translator.

Rose Elizabeth Cleveland.

January 22, 1910.

THE SOLILOQUIES OF ST. AUGUSTINE
BOOK I
I

1. For many days I had been debating within myself many and diverse things, seeking constantly, and with anxiety, to find out my real self, my best good, and the evil to be avoided, when suddenly one — I know not, but eagerly strive to know, whether it were myself or another, within me or without — said to me:

R.   Now consider: suppose you had discovered something concerning that which you are so constantly and anxiously seeking to know; to what would you entrust it, in order that you might give your attention to things following?

A.   To memory, of course.

R.   Is the memory an adequate custodian of all things which the mind discovers?

A.   Hardly; in fact it cannot be.

R.   Such things must, then, be written down. But how will you do this, when your health *Endnote 001* does not admit of the labor of writing them? They cannot be dictated, for they demand absolute solitude.

A.   What you say is true, and so I do not see how I am to proceed without embarrassment.

R.   Pray *Endnote 002* for health and help in accomplishing your desires, and write this prayer down also, that by these first fruits you may become more courageous. Then summarize briefly the conclusions at which you have arrived. Do not make any effort to attract a crowd of readers; a few of your own townsmen will suffice.

A.   I will do as you advise.

2. O God, Founder of the Universe, help me, that, first of all, I may pray aright: and next, that I may act as one worthy to be heard by Thee: and, finally, set me free. *Endnote 003* God, through whom all things are, which of themselves could have no being; God, who dost not permit that to perish, whose tendency it is to destroy itself! God, who hast created out of nothing *Endnote 004* this world, which the eyes of all perceive to be most beautiful! *Endnote 005* God, who dost not cause evil, but dost cause that it shall not become the worst! God, who dost reveal to those few fleeing for refuge to that which truly is, that evil *Endnote 006* is nothing! God, through whom the Universe, even with its perverse part, is perfect! *Endnote 007* God, to whom dissonance is nothing, since in the end the worst resolves into harmony with the better! *Endnote 008* God, whom every creature capable of loving, loves, whether consciously or unconsciously!

God, in whom all things are, yet whom the shame of no creature in the universe disgraces, nor his malice harms, nor his error misleads! God, who dost not permit any save the pure *Endnote 009* to know the true! God, Father of Truth, Father of Wisdom, Father of the True and Perfect Life, Father of Blessedness, Father of the Good and the Beautiful, Father of Intelligible Light, *Endnote 010* Father of our awakening and enlightening, Father of that pledge which warns us to return to Thee!

3. Thee do I invoke, God, Truth, in whom and by whom and through whom are all things true which are true: God, Wisdom, in whom and by whom and through whom are all

wise who are wise: God, true and perfect Life, in whom and by whom and through whom those live who do truly and perfectly live: God, Blessedness, in whom and by whom and through whom are all blessed who are blessed: God, the Good and the Beautiful, in whom and by whom and through whom are all things good and beautiful, which are good and beautiful: God, Intelligible Light, in whom and by whom all shine intelligibly, who do intelligibly shine: God, whose kingdom is that whole realm unknown to sense: God, from whose kingdom law for even these lower realms is derived: God, from whom to turn is to fall; to whom to turn is to rise; in whom to abide is to stand: God, from whom to go out is to waste away; unto whom to return is to revive; in whom to dwell is to live: *Endnote 011* God, whom no one, unless deceived, loses: whom no one, unless admonished, seeks: whom no one, unless purified, finds: God, whom to abandon is to perish; whom to long for is to love; whom to see is to possess: God, to whom Faith excites, Hope uplifts, Love joins: God, through whom we overcome the enemy, Thee do I supplicate!

God, whose gift it is that we do not utterly perish: God, by whom we are warned to watch: God, through whom we discriminate good things from evil things: God, through whom we flee from evil and follow after good: God, through whom we yield not to adversity: God, through whom we both serve well and rule well: God, through whom we discern that certain things we had deemed essential to ourselves are truly foreign to us, while those we had deemed foreign to us are essential: God, through whom we are not held fast by the baits and seductions of the wicked: God, through whom the decrease of our possessions does not diminish us: God, through whom our better part is not subject to our worse: God, through whom death is swallowed up in victory! God, who dost turn us about in the way: God, who dost strip us of that which is not, and clothe us with that which is: God, who dost make us worthy of being heard: God, who dost defend us: God, who dost lead us into all truth: God, who dost speak all good things to us: God, who dost not deprive us of sanity nor permit another to do so: God, who dost recall us to the path: God, who dost lead us to the door: God, who dost cause that it is open to those who knock: God, who givest us the bread of Life: God, through whom we thirst for that water, which having drunk, we shall never thirst again: God, who dost convince the world of sin, of righteousness, and of judgment: God, through whom the unbelief of others doth not move us: God, through whom we reprobate the error of those who deem that souls have no deserving in Thy sight: God, through whom we are not in bondage to weak and beggarly elements: God, who dost purify and prepare us for divine rewards, propitious, come Thou to me!

4. In whatever I say do Thou come to my help, O Thou one God, one true Eternal Substance, where is no discord, no confusion, no change, no want, no death: where is all harmony, all illumination, all steadfastness, all abundance, all life: where nothing is lacking and nothing redundant; where Begetter and Begotten are one: God, whom all things serve which do serve and whom every good soul obeys! God, by whose laws the poles rotate, the stars pursue their courses, the sun leads on the day, the moon tempers the night, and the whole order of the Universe — through days by the alternations of light and darkness; through months by the waxing and waning of moons; through years by the successions of spring, summer, autumn and winter; through cycles by the completing of the sun's course; through vast eons of time by the return of the stars to their first risings — preserves by these unvarying repetitions of periods, so far as sensible matter may, the marvellous immutability of things; God, by whose laws forever standing, the unstable motion of mutable things is not allowed to fall into confusion and is, throughout the circling ages, recalled by curb and bit to the semblance of stability: by whose laws the will of the soul is free, *Endnote 012* and rewards to the good, and penalties to the wicked, are everywhere distributed by unchangeable necessity:

God, by whom all good flows toward us, all evil is driven from us: God, above whom, outside whom, without whom, is nothing: God, beneath whom, in whom, with whom, is everything: who hast made man after Thine own image *Endnote 013* and likeness, which he who knows himself discovers: Hear, hear, hear me! My God, my master, my king, my father, my cause, my hope, my wealth, my honor, my home, my country, *Endnote 014* my salvation, my light, my life! Hear, hear, hear me, in that way of Thine, known best to few!

5. At last I love Thee alone, Thee alone follow, Thee alone seek, Thee alone am I ready to serve: for Thou alone, by right, art ruler; under Thy rule *Endnote 015* do I wish to be. Command, I pray, and order what Thou wilt, but heal and open my ears that I may hear Thy commands, heal and open my eyes that I may see Thy nod; cast all unsoundness from me that I may recognize Thee! Tell me whither to direct my gaze that I may look upon Thee, and I hope that I shall do all things which Thou commandest!

Receive, I pray, Master and most merciful Father, me, Thy Fugitive! *Endnote 016* I have suffered already enough punishment, long enough been in bondage to Thine enemies whom Thou hast under Thy feet, long enough been the sport of delusions.

Receive me, Thy household servant, fleeing from them, for even these received me, though alien to them, fleeing from Thee! I feel that I ought to return to Thee: let Thy door open to me knocking: teach me, Thou, how to come to Thee! I have nothing other than the will: I know nothing other than that the fleeting and the falling should be spurned, the fixed and eternal sought after. This do I, Father, for this is all I know: but how to make my way to Thee I know not. Do Thou suggest it, make it plain, equip me for the journey!

If they who take refuge in Thee find Thee by faith, give me faith! if by virtue, give me virtue! if by knowledge, give me knowledge! Increase my faith, increase my hope, increase my charity, O Goodness of Thine, unique and admirable!

6. After Thee am I groping, and by whatsoever things Thou mayest be felt after, even these do I seek from Thee! For if Thou desert a man, he perishes: but Thou desertest him not, for Thou art the sum of good, and no man, seeking Thee aright, has failed to find Thee; and every one seeks Thee aright whom Thou dost cause to so seek Thee. Cause me, O Father, to seek Thee; let me not stray from the path, and to me, seeking Thee, let nothing befall in place of Thyself! If I desire nothing beside Thyself, let me, I implore, find Thee now; but if there is in me the desire for something beside Thyself, do Thou Thyself purify me, and make me fit to look upon Thee!

For the rest, whatever concerns the welfare of this mortal body of mine, so long as I do not know how it may serve either myself or those I love, to Thee, Father, wisest and best, do I commit it, and I pray that Thou wilt admonish me concerning it as shall be needful. But this I do implore Thy most excellent mercy, that Thou convert me in my inmost self to Thee, and, as I incline toward Thee, let nothing oppose; and command that so long as I endure and care for this same body, I may be pure and magnanimous and just and prudent, a perfect lover and learner of Thy wisdom, a fit inhabitant of a dwelling place in Thy most blessed Kingdom!

Amen and Amen! *Endnote 017*

II

7. A.   Behold, I have prayed to God.

R.   What, then, do you desire to know?

A.   Those things for which I have prayed.

R.   Sum them up, briefly.

A.   I desire to know God and the soul.

R.   And nothing more?

A.   Nothing whatever. *Endnote 018*

R.   Begin then to seek. But first make clear to me how God may be so demonstrated to you that you can say: "It is enough."

A.   I do not know how he can be so demonstrated to me that I can say, "It is enough"; for I believe that I know nothing in the way that I wish to know God.

R.   What, then, are we to do? For do you not consider that it must first be known what it is to know God sufficiently, so that, when you have attained to that much knowledge, you need seek no further?

A.   I do indeed think so, but by what plan it shall become possible to do this, I do not perceive. For what have I ever known which is like God so that I could say: "As I know this, so do I desire to know God!"

R.   Having known nothing like God, from what source do you know that you have not yet known Him?

A.   Because, should I have known anything like God, I would, without doubt, love it; but, as it is, I love only God and the soul, and know neither the one nor the other.

R.   Do you not, then, love your friends?

A.   How, loving the soul, should I not love them?

R.   Is it in this way, then, that you love gnats and bugs?

A.   I said that I love, not animals, but the soul.

R.   Either, then, your friends are not men or you love them not; for every man is an animal, and you say you do not love animals.

A.   They are men and I love them, not in that they are animals, but in that they are men: that is, from the fact that they possess rational souls, which I love even in thieves. For it is permitted me to love reason in anything whatever, although I may justly hate him who makes a bad use of it. So much the more, then, do I love my friends, by as much as they make a good use of that rational soul, or as much, indeed, as they desire to do so. *Endnote 019*

III

8. R.   I accept this, but yet if some one should say to you, I will cause you to know God as well as you know Alypius, *Endnote 020* would you not thank him and say: "That is enough"?

A.   I would indeed thank him, but I would not say: "That is enough."

R.   And why, may I ask?

R.   Because I do not know God even as I know Alypius, and I do not know Alypius well enough.

R.   See to it, then, that you are not arrogant in desiring to know God well enough — you who do not even know Alypius well enough!

A.   That does not follow. For, in comparison with the stars, what is more trifling a matter than my dinner? Yet, while I do not know what I shall have to-morrow for dinner, and am wholly ignorant of that, I do not deem it arrogant to affirm that I do know in what sign the moon will rise.

R.   Will you, then, be satisfied to know God after the fashion in which you know in what sign the moon will rise to-morrow?

A.   No, that is not enough, for it is by my senses that this is known. Also I know not whether God, or some occult natural cause, might not suddenly change the ordinary course of the moon, and if this should happen, all that I had taken for granted would become false.

R.   And do you believe this could happen? *Endnote 021*

A.   I do not. But I seek what I may know, not what I may believe. For it may, indeed, be truly said that we believe all that we know, but not that we know everything that we believe.

R.   Do you, then, in your present undertaking, reject all testimony of the senses?

A.   I do altogether.

R.   How about your intimate friend, whom you have said you know only partially; do you know him by sense or by intellect?

A.   The knowledge which I have of him by sense — if indeed anything is truly known by sense — is worthless and is enough: that part by which he is truly my friend is the mind itself, and I wish to pursue that by the intellect.

R.   And can he not otherwise be known?

A.   In no other way.

R.   Do you venture, then, to declare that your friend, and he, too, your most intimate friend, is unknown to you?

A.   And why should I not venture? For I consider that a most just law of friendship which prescribes that one shall love his friend, not less, and not more, than himself. Therefore, since I do not know myself, what reproach can it be to me that I declare him to be unknown to me, especially since, as I believe, he does not really know himself?

R.   If, then, those things which you desire to know are such as are pursued by the intellect, when I said that, since you did not even know Alypius, you were arrogant in desiring to know God, you should not have cited your dinner and the moon as illustrations, since these, as you have said, pertain to sense.

IV

9. But how does that concern us? Now answer me: It those things which Plato and Plotinus said *Endnote 022* concerning God are true, is it enough for you to know God as they knew Him?

A.   It does not necessarily follow that, even if those things which they said are true, they knew them to be so. For many persons discourse most fluently of things of which they are ignorant, as I, just now in prayer, have desired to know many things, which, although I have mentioned them, I would not desire to know if I already knew them. But am I, therefore, the less able to mention them? For I have given utterance, not to things which my intellect comprehends, but which, gathered here and there, and committed to the memory, I have reinforced by all the faith of which I am capable. But to know is another thing.

R.   Tell me now, I beg: do you, at least, know what, in the science of Geometry, a line is?

A.   That I certainly do know.

R.   And do you not, in this admission, stand in awe of the Academicians?

A.   Not at all. For it is the wise whom they forbid to err, and I am not wise. At this point, therefore, I do not fear to admit the knowledge of such things as I know. When, as I desire, I shall have attained to Wisdom I will do as she shall exhort. *Endnote 023*

R.   I do not object: but I was going to ask if you know the ball which is called a sphere in the same way as you know a line?

A.   I do.

R.   And do you know one as well as the other, or one more or less than the other?

A.   I know both equally, for in nothing am I deceived in either.

R.   And have you perceived these by the senses or by the intellect?

A.   In this matter my experience with the senses has been as with a ship: for when they had carried me where I was going, and I had dismissed them, and was as if placed on dry land, and had begun to turn these matters over in thought, I was, for a long time, unsteady of foot. Wherefore it seems to me that one could sooner swim on dry land than perceive geometrical truths by the senses, although in learning the rudiments they are of some use.

R.   You do not, then, hesitate to call your acquaintance, such as it is, with these things knowledge?

A.   No, if the Stoics, who ascribe knowledge only to the wise, permit. I certainly do not deny that I have such perception of these things as they concede even to the unwise. But I do not indeed very much fear the Stoics. I hold these things concerning which you have been asking in positive knowledge. *Endnote 024* Go on, then, that I may see your purpose in these questions.

R.   Do not be in haste; we have time enough. Be very cautious what you accept, lest you concede something rashly. I am studying to make you happy *Endnote 025* in the certainty of things in which you will fear no downfall, while you, as if this were an easy matter, demand that I make haste.

A.   May God cause it to be as you say! Question now as you will, and if I repeat this offense rebuke me more severely.

10. R.   Very well. Is it clear to you that it is impossible to divide a line lengthways?

A.   It is clear.

R.   How about crossways?

A.   That, of course, can be done to infinity.

R.   And is it equally obvious that it is impossible for two equal circles to be on one side of a sphere, equi-distant from the center?

A.   It is.

R.   And do the line and the sphere seem one and the same thing to you, or do they differ somewhat?

A.   Who would not see that they differ greatly?

R.   Since, then, you have an equal knowledge of each notwithstanding that, as you say, they differ greatly, it follows that although objects of knowledge differ, yet the knowledge by which one is known is identical with the knowledge by which the other is known.

A.   Who has denied that?

R.   You, yourself, a little time ago. For, when I asked you how you desired to know God, so that you might say: "It is enough"; you replied that you were unable to say, for the reason that among the things you know there is nothing like God. How, then! The line and the sphere, — are they alike?

A.   Who could say that?

R.   But I had not asked what you knew like God, but what you know in the same way as you desire to know God. For, though the line and the sphere are in no way similar, yet your knowing of the one is identical with your knowing of the other. Wherefore tell me: would it be enough for you to know God, as you know the sphere of Geometry, that is, to doubt nothing concerning God as you doubt nothing concerning it?

V

11. A. I answer you, that, however vehemently you urge and argue, I do not, nevertheless, dare to say that I desire to know God as I know these things. For not only do these things, that is, the sphere and God, differ, but the knowing of the one cannot be the same as the knowing of the other. In the first place, the line and the sphere do not differ so much that one science may not treat of each, while no Geometry has professed to treat of God. And, in the second place, were my knowledge of these things of the same sort as is the knowledge which I desire to have of God, I should rejoice that I know them as much as I expect to rejoice in the cognition of God. But now I more than despise these things in comparison with Him; and it seems to me, that, should I attain to the cognition of Him, and see Him in the way He can be seen, *Endnote 026* these things would perish from my memory altogether. Indeed, even now, it is an effort to recall these to mind, because of my absorbing desire for Him.

R. Be it so, then, that the knowledge of God would rejoice you very much more than the knowledge of these inferior things: yet this fact does not result from the unlikeness of their apprehension. Or is it by one kind of seeing you gaze upon the earth and by another upon the tranquil sky, since the sight of the latter charms you so much more than that of the former? And, the eyes being trustworthy, if you were asked whether you were as sure that you had looked upon the earth as upon the sky, you would reply that you were, although not so delighting in the aspect of the earth as in the beauty and splendor of the sky.

A. This illustration, I confess, moves me, and I am constrained to agree, that, as much in kind as the earth differs from the heavens, so much do the demonstrations of the sciences, though certain and exact, differ from the intelligible majesty of God.

VI

12. R.   It is well that you are thus moved. For Reason, who speaks to you, promises that God ^{Endnote 027} Himself shall be even so demonstrated to your mind as is the sun to your eyes. For the eyes of the mind are the senses of the soul. Now the truths of science are made visible to the mind, as the light of the sun makes visible to the eyes the earth and terrestrial objects. But it is God Himself who shines. ^{Endnote 028} And I, Reason, am such to the mind as is sight to the eyes: for to have eyes that you may look is one thing, and to so look that you may see is another. And so it is that the task of the soul is three-fold, that it possess eyes fit for use, that it look, that it see. Now the eyes of the soul are fit when she is pure from every fleshly taint, that is, when all desire of mortal things is purged and far away, which task Faith alone is, at the outset, equal to. For this cannot be made manifest to a soul marred and diseased by lust, since unless sound she cannot see, nor will she apply herself to the labor of making herself sound if she does not believe, that, when so, she will be able to see. And, furthermore, though one may have this Faith and believe that the matter is as has been stated, and that his ability to see can come about only in this way, yet if he despair of recovery, will he not give himself up, and despise and disobey the orders of his physician?

A.   That is perfectly true, especially since one who is ill of necessity feels these orders to be severe.

R.   Hope, then, must be added to Faith.

A.   I believe so.

R.   And how if the soul have this Faith, and also Hope that she can be healed, and yet does not love nor desire the promised Light, but is constrained from long habit, which has made them pleasant, to deem it her duty to abide content with her shadows, will she not none the less reject her physician?

A.   She will forthwith.

R.   Therefore a third, Charity, is needed!

A.   Nothing is so absolutely necessary.

R.   Without, then, these three, no soul is sound enough to see, that is, to cognize her God?

13. When, then, you shall have sound eyes, what remains?

A.   That the soul look.

R.   The gaze of the soul is Reason; but since it does not follow that every one who looks, sees, that right and perfect looking, which is followed by seeing, is called Virtue, for Virtue is rectified and perfected Reason. But that very act of looking, even though the eyes be sound, cannot turn them toward the Light unless three things persist: Faith — by which the soul believes that, that toward which the gaze has been directed, is such that to gaze upon it will cause blessedness: Hope — by which, the eyes being rightly fixed, the soul expects this vision to follow: and Love — which is the soul's longing to see and to enjoy it. Such looking is followed by the vision of God Himself, who is the goal of the soul's gaze, not because it could not continue to look, but because there is nothing beyond this on which it can fix its gaze. This is truly perfected Reason — Virtue — attaining its proper end, on which the happy life follows. And this intellectual vision is that which is in the soul a conjunction of the seer and the seen: as seeing with the eyes results from the conjunction of the sense of sight and the sensible object, either of which being lacking, nothing can be seen.

VII

14. When now it has come about that the soul sees, that is, intellectually apprehends God, let us see whether these three things are still necessary to her. How shall Faith be necessary when the soul has now sight? Or Hope, since it has the thing hoped for? Charity alone is nothing diminished, but rather, indeed, very greatly augmented. For when the soul shall have seen this true and unique beauty she will love it the more, and unless with mighty love she fix upon it her gaze, nor turn it thence to anything whatever, she cannot abide in this most blessed vision. But even while the soul is in the body, *Endnote 029* although it may behold most fully, that is, may apprehend God, nevertheless since the senses of the body serve in their own proper office, though they may cause doubt, they cannot cause delusion, and that which opposes them and believes rather that which is contrary to them to be true, may, so far, be called Faith. Again, since God being apprehended, the soul may in this lower life attain blessedness, yet because she must still suffer much molestation by the flesh, she must hope that after death all these troubles will cease to exist. Neither, therefore, may Hope desert the soul in this life; but when, after this life, the soul shall have found herself complete in God, Love, by which she is held there, abides; for she cannot be said to still have Faith that these things are true, since she is solicited by no intrusion of the false; nor that aught remains to be hoped for, since she now possesses all securely. Three things, then, concern the soul: that she be sound, that she look, that she see. Another three, Faith, Hope and Charity, are all needful for health of soul, and Reason's gaze; while for the vision itself, all, indeed while in the body; but, after this life, Charity alone. *Endnote 030*

VIII

15. Be attentive now, while, so far as is at present necessary, I disclose to you by similitude of sensible objects, some truth concerning even God Himself. God, undoubtedly, is intelligible even as are these obvious intelligibilities of science; with, however, a wide difference. For the earth is visible and light is visible, but the earth cannot be seen unless made visible by light. So is it with those things treated of by the sciences, which he who apprehends concedes to be most true, and yet it is not credible that they can be apprehended, unless made manifest by some illumination, by some other sun, as it were their own. Thus, as of the sensible sun, we may predicate three things: namely, that it is, that it shines, that it makes objects visible; even so may we predicate three things of that most mysterious God whom you long to know: viz., that He is, that He is apprehended, that He causes other things to be apprehended. These two things, i. e. yourself and God, I dare to teach you. Now tell me how you receive these things: as probabilities or as truths?

A.   As probabilities, obviously, and I am stimulated, I admit, to hope for something more. For, excepting those two statements concerning the line and the sphere, nothing has been said by you which I should venture so far as to declare absolute knowledge.

R.   That is not to be wondered at, for, so far, nothing has been so demonstrated as to compel your recognition.

IX

16. But why do we loiter? The journey should be pursued. Now let us see whether we are in a sound condition, for that is the first step.

A.   It is for you to find, if, either in myself or in yourself, anything can be detected. I will reply to your question so far as I am conscious of anything.

R.   Do you love anything beside the knowledge of God and of yourself?

A.   As I now feel, I can answer, "nothing:" but it is safer to say "I do not know." For it has frequently been my experience, when I did not believe it possible to be moved by anything else, yet, something coming into my mind would disturb me far beyond what I had believed possible. And again, although something passing through my mind as a mere suggestion would not much disturb me, yet the very fact of its coming did disturb me more than I had supposed: but it now seems to me that I can be disturbed by only three things, namely: the fear of losing those I love, the fear of pain, and the fear of death.

R.   You love, then, life in the companionship of those dearest to you, your own good health, and your life itself in the flesh; for, were it not so, you would not fear their loss?

A.   I confess it is so.

R.   The sole fact, then, that your friends are not all with you, and that your health is not wholly sound, occasions you some distress of mind, for that, I see, must follow.

A.   You see rightly; I cannot deny it.

R.   How if you should suddenly feel and become certain that you were sound of body, and should see all those whom you love enjoying together with yourself ease and plenty; would you be almost transported with joy?

A.   Almost, indeed. Nay! If this, of all other things, might, as you say, suddenly fall to my lot, how could I contain myself, or how conceal my excess of joy? *Endnote 031*

R.   You are, therefore, even now, agitated by all diseases and perturbations of the mind. What impudence is it, then, that such eyes should wish to look upon that Sun!

A.   You come to your conclusions as if I did not feel precisely how far my health has improved, or what plague has retreated and what still holds its ground. Prove that to be true!

X

17. R.   Are you not aware that the eyes of the body, even though sound, being frequently hurt and turned away by the light of this sensible sun, flee for refuge to shade? So you are thinking over your improvement, not of that which you desire to see! nor yet of this discussion, how you consider us to have advanced: — Do you not desire riches?

A.   They are not, now, my first object. I am now three and thirty years of age, and I have ceased to desire riches for almost fourteen years, nor, if they happened to be offered to me, would I have any other interest in them, save such as a freeman requires for his maintenance and use. A single book of Cicero's *Endnote 032* immediately and easily persuaded me that riches should not be craved, but if they fell to our lot should be wisely and carefully administered.

R.   What about honors? *Endnote 033*

A.   These, I confess, I have but recently ceased to wish for.

R.   And how about a wife? Would not one beautiful, modest, docile and cultivated, or at least, one who could be easily taught by yourself, bringing, also, — since you despise opulence, — a marriage portion sufficient to prevent her being a tax upon your leisure, especially if you might confidently hope that no annoyance could come to you because of her, would not such a wife greatly delight you?

A.   No matter how you portray her or load her with desirable things, I have decided that nothing is so much to be shunned as sexual relations, for I feel that nothing so much casts down the mind of man from its citadel as do the blandishments of women, and that physical contact without which a wife cannot be possessed. Therefore if it pertain to the office of a wise man (and I am not yet sure that it does) to give himself the care of a family, whoever sustains the marriage relation for the sake of this alone is, I may indeed concede, to be admired, but not, therefore, to be imitated; for the attempt has in it more of peril than the event can have of satisfaction. Enough, however, that for the sake of my freedom of mind, I have, and as I believe, rightly and usefully, decided neither to desire, nor seek, nor take a wife.

R.   I do not now ask what you have resolved upon, but whether at the present time you have actually overcome sexual desire itself, or whether you still struggle against it? For this concerns the soundness of your eyes.

A.   I now neither seek nor desire anything whatever of this sort. It is with horror and loathing that I even remember it. What more can you ask? And this good increases in me every day. For, as much as the hope of seeing that Superior Beauty, for which I am so consumed by vehement desire, increases, so much does all desire and delight converge to that direction. *Endnote 034*

R.   And now about the enjoyment of food: how much does that concern you?

A.   As to those things which I have cut off from my diet, they do not disturb me; those still allowed I enjoy when before me, yet so that even they could be entirely withdrawn without causing me any annoyance. When they are not immediately present, the appetite for them does not dare to intrude itself, as an impediment to my thoughts. But ask me no more concerning food or drink or baths, or any other pleasure of the flesh. I desire to have them only in proportion to the benefit they can confer upon my health. *Endnote 035*

18. R.   You have made great progress. Nevertheless some things remain which greatly hinder the seeing of that Light. But I now attempt something which it seems to me easy to find out; for either nothing remains to be overcome, or, of all these things which we believe to have been eradicated, the root infection still remains; — in which case we have made no progress whatever. Now I ask you whether, if you were persuaded that not otherwise than by an ample competence equal to the supply of all your mutual necessities, would it be possible for you to pursue the study of Wisdom in company with your many very dear friends, would you not choose and desire riches?

A.   I admit that I would.

R.   And how, if it should be shown that, your authority being increased by public honors, you could persuade many to be wise, and that your intimate friends themselves could not curb their worldly desires and turn wholly to seeking after God, unless they themselves should become persons of consequence; and that this, except by your own importance and dignity, could not be accomplished, would not these material things be greatly to be desired and urgently to be sought after?

A.   It is as you say.

R.   Now concerning a wife: I will not argue, for perhaps there can exist no such necessity that she should be taken. If, however, by means of her ample patrimony, it were possible that all those whom you desire to have live with you in one place, could be comfortably supported, herself also cordially agreeing to this arrangement, and if, especially, by reason of nobility of birth, she were of sufficient influence to bring within easy reach of you those honors which you have just now admitted to be necessary, — I do not know whether it would be proper for you to despise these things.

A.   How should I dare to hope for such things? *Endnote 036*

19. R.   You speak as if I were asking what you hope for. I am not now asking what, among things denied, would displease you: but what, being offered, would please you. A dead plague is one thing, a sleeping one another. And here this saying of certain learned men is pertinent: "all fools are mad, as all dunghills stink, yet one does not always realize this fact, but only when they are stirred up." *Endnote 037* It is of the greatest importance to us whether carnal desire is stupefied by despair of satisfaction, or expelled by health of mind. *Endnote 038*

A.   Although I cannot make any answer to this, yet you will never persuade me that, in the inclination of mind which I now feel to be mine, I am to believe I have made no progress.

R.   I believe that this seems so to you because, although it is possible that you should wish for such things, it would, nevertheless, not be for their own sake, but for some other reason, that they would appear desirable to you.

A.   This is what I have been wishing to say: for as to riches, when, formerly, I desired them, it was because I wished to be rich; and honors, the desire for which I have admitted did, until recently, dominate me, I was wont to wish for because of I know not what glamour about them which fascinated me. And when I sought a wife, I sought her for nothing else than for the sake of getting pleasure without loss of reputation. There was then in me a desire for these things in themselves, but I now absolutely spurn them all. Yet, if these things which I do long for can be reached only through those, I seek them, not that they may be fondly treasured but submissively tolerated. *Endnote 039*

R.   Excellent! For I do not consider that those things which are asked for solely on account of something else can be said to be desired at all.

XII

20. R.   But now I ask you why you desire that those men whom you love should live with you, or should live at all?

A.   In order that we may together inquire into God and our own souls. For thus, he who first found out something could, without labor, easily impart it to the others.

R.   But how if they do not care to inquire into these things?

A.   I will persuade them so that they will care to.

R.   But suppose you are not able to do this, either because they have already themselves made these discoveries, or deem them to be things which cannot be discovered; or because they are preoccupied with the cares and desires of other things.

A.   I will still keep hold of them and they of me, as if we were able.

R.   But suppose their presence is really an impediment to you in your researches. Would not that embarrass you; and if they cannot be otherwise, would you not prefer to be alone rather than so situated?

A.   I confess that I would. *Endnote 040*

R.   You do not then crave either that they live or live with you, save for the purpose of finding Wisdom? *Endnote 041*

A.   Such is the case.

R.   And how if your own life were proved to be an impediment to the attainment of Wisdom — would you wish it to continue?

A.   I would flee from it forthwith. *Endnote 042*

R.   And suppose that you were shown that whether in or out of the body you could equally well attain to Wisdom, would you care whether here or in another life you should enjoy that which you delight in?

A.   If I might rest assured that nothing worse were in store for me hereafter, and no backward step from that to which I have already advanced, I would not care.

R.   You fear then to die, lest you shall be involved in some worse evil by which the knowledge of God shall be taken away from you?

A.   Such as I have conceived it, not only do I fear lest it shall be taken away from me, but also lest the entrance upon those things, at sight of which I stand marvelling, shall be closed to me; although what I now grasp will, I trust, remain with me.

R.   You desire then that life shall remain to you, not on its own account but on account of Wisdom?

A.   So it is.

21. R.   Fear of pain remains, which probably moves you by its own intrinsic power.

A.   Even that I do not very greatly fear on any other account than because it hinders me in my researches. Not long since, although I was tormented with a very severe toothache, *Endnote 043* so that I was unable to do any continuous thinking, except on subjects with which I was already familiar, and was altogether prevented from undertaking any researches in which concentration of mind was necessary, yet, even then, it seemed to me that should that Illumination disclose itself to my mind, I should either lose all consciousness of the pain, or would certainly support it as if it were nothing. Up to this time I have had no more serious pain to bear, but since frequently realizing how much more intolerable pain might fall to my lot, I am constrained to agree with Cornelius Celsus, when he says that the greatest good is wisdom, and the greatest evil physical pain. Nor does the argument for this saying seem to me absurd. For, he says, since we are compounded of two parts, namely, of mind and body, the superior part is the mind and the inferior the body: and the greatest good is the best of the better part, and the greatest evil the worst of the worst part, and wisdom is the best thing in the soul and pain the worst in the body. Therefore he concludes, as I think not at all falsely, that the greatest good is to be wise, the greatest evil to suffer pain.

R.   Later on we will see about that. For perhaps Wisdom herself, toward whom we are urging our way, will persuade us otherwise. If, however, this is shown to be true, we will, doubtless, entertain the same opinion as to the greatest good and the greatest evil.

XIII

22. Now let us inquire what kind of a lover you are of that Wisdom, whom, with most chaste regard and embrace and with no interposing veil, but as if nude, in a way she does not permit save to very few of her most favored suitors, you desire to grasp and to gaze upon. For surely were you consumed with desire for some most beautiful woman, it would be but just that she should not yield herself to you, if she had discovered that another beside herself were loved by you. Nor will this most chaste beauty of Wisdom disclose herself to you, except you are consumed by desire for her alone.

A.   Why then am I, unhappy I, so long kept waiting in suspense and excruciating agony? Surely I have proved that I love no other, for that which is not loved for itself is not loved at all. But Wisdom I love for herself alone, and other things — life, leisure, friends — which I wish to have in addition, I fear to be without, on her account only. How boundless must be the love I bear to that Beauty, when not only do I not envy other lovers, but even seek many more who may with me long for her; with me gaze, marvelling, upon her; with me lay hold upon, with me enjoy her; so much the more shall they be my friends, as she shall be loved by us in common!

23. R.   It is altogether fitting that such should the lovers of Wisdom be. She, union with whom is pure and without contamination, seeks such. But she is not won in one way alone. *Endnote 044* It is according to his soundness and strength that each one comes to know this unique and most veritable good. There is an intellectual illumination of an ineffable and mysterious sort. *Endnote 045* Ordinary light may, so far as it can, teach us something concerning that higher Light. There are eyes so vigorous and sound as, though scarcely open, to turn full upon the sun without shrinking. To such, light is, in a way, health itself, nor do they need a physician, save only perhaps for advice. To such it is enough to believe, to hope, to love. But there are others whose eyes are hurt by that very effulgence which they so vehemently long to look upon, and often turning from it go with delight back to their shadows. Such as these may be truly said to be sound, but no attempt to show them that which they are not able to look upon is without danger. They need first to be exercised by a salutary encouragement of desire, and an equally wise postponement of its satisfaction.

They should, first, be shown some things which are not in themselves luminous, but can be seen only by reflected light, such as a garment or a wall, or anything of that sort. After that, something else, which, though not itself luminous, yet glows with more beauty by reflection than does the former, as gold or silver or something similar; but not so brightly as to hurt the eye. Next, they should look upon some moderate terrestrial fire, then upon the stars, then the moon, then the glow of dawn, and the growing splendor of sunrise. And whoever accustoms himself to these things, whether in unbroken order, or with some omissions, will come to look upon the sun itself without shrinking and with great delight. The most excellent teachers use some such method as this with those eagerly desirous of Wisdom, who already see, but whose sight is not acute. For it is the office of good discipline to attain Wisdom by a certain order of approach, and without that order *Endnote 046* it is scarcely credible that the approach can be happy. But we have, I think, written enough for to-day. Health must be considered.

24. Another day having arrived: —

A.   Give now if you can, I beg, I implore, this order. Proceed; do what you will, by any means, in any way. Command things however difficult, however arduous, and, nevertheless, if they are within my power, I shall certainly, through them, attain to that which I desire.

R.   One thing alone can I teach you; nothing else do I know: *Endnote 047* the things of sense must be abandoned, and the greatest caution must be used, so long as we carry about this body, lest some adhesive impediment of sense should clog our wings, whose task, when whole and perfect, it is to bear us upward away from these shadows to that higher Light, which it befits not to disclose itself to those shut up in this cave, *Endnote 048* unless they shall have been such, that, when they escape, their prison being either rent asunder or decayed away, they shall be able to mount up to their native atmospheres. And so, when you shall have become such, that nothing whatever of earth can charm you, in that very moment, in that very instant of time, believe me, you shall look upon that which you desire. *Endnote 049*

A.   When, then, shall that be, I pray you? For I do not think it possible to arrive at that complete contempt of these inferior things, until I shall have first beheld that in comparison with which they become vile.

25. R.   This is as if the eyes of the body should say: "When I shall have seen the sun, I will no longer love darkness." For, though it seems right that this should be the order by which to proceed, it is, in fact, a long way from it. For the eye loves darkness for the very reason that it is not sound, and yet, unless sound, it cannot gaze upon the sun. The mind is often deceived in this, and boasting and thinking itself sound, as if it had occasion, it complains that it does not see. But that Beauty knows when it should disclose itself; for she, herself, assumes the office of physician, and knows better who may be fit to look upon her than do they themselves who are made fit.

Thus we, having emerged so far, seem to ourselves to see; but how deep we have been sunk or to what point we have risen, we are not permitted to either feel or think; and so, because we have not a worse disease, we conclude that we have none. Do you not observe how, only yesterday, we announced, as if secure, that we were no longer hindered by any fleshly plague, and that we loved Wisdom alone, and sought for and desired other things on her account only? How worthless, how foul, how execrable, how horrible, seemed to you a woman's embrace, as we were inquiring between ourselves concerning the desire for a wife! And yet, that very night, being wakeful, when we again discussed the same matter, how far other you felt than you would have supposed, when thrilled with these imagined blandishments and that amorous softness! — far less, indeed, than its wont, but yet, far otherwise than you had been asserting. May that most confidential physician of yours therefore demonstrate to you both what, by his care, you have escaped, and what yet remains to be cured!

26. A.   Silence, I beseech you, silence! Why do you so torment me; why probe so deep? Now I weep beyond endurance! Henceforth I promise nothing, I presume nothing, lest you ask again concerning these things. You say truly that He whom I ardently desire to see will, Himself, know when I am restored to health. Let Him do what pleases Him; let Him disclose Himself when it pleases Him! I now commit myself wholly to His care and clemency. For I believe, for all time, He will not cease to uplift to Himself those so inclined. I will pronounce nothing concerning my soundness until I shall have looked upon that Beauty. *Endnote 050*

R.   May you indeed do nothing other. But now restrain yourself from tears and gird up your mind. You have wept overmuch, and the pain in your chest is seriously affected by it.

A.   Would you set a bound to my tears when I can see no bound to my misery? Or do you bid me consider the health of my body when my real self may be consumed with infection? Nay, I implore you, if you are of any avail for me, that you endeavor to lead me onward by some less tedious route, that, by some proximity of that Light, which, if I have advanced somewhat, I am now able to bear, it will shame my eyes to return to those shadows I have left; if, indeed, those things can be said to be abandoned which can still venture to cajole my blindness.

XV

27. R.   Let us, if you please, conclude this first volume that we may set out upon a second by some propitious way; for this inclination of yours must not cease for want of suitable exercise.

A.   I refuse absolutely to consent that this little book shall be concluded until you shall have opened to me some little glimmer concerning the nearness of that Light on which I am intent.

R.   Your Divine Healer consents to grant you this much: for I know not what effulgence touches me and invites me to lead you thither. Be, therefore, intently receptive.

A.   Lead on; seize and hurry me whither you will.

R.   Do you affirm truly that you will to cognize God and the soul?

A.   Such is my whole concern.

R.   And nothing more?

A.   Absolutely nothing.

R.   What! Do you not desire to comprehend Truth?

A.   As if I could truly have acquaintance with these except through that!

R.   That, then, must first be cognized, in order that these may be.

A.   I agree to that.

R.   Let us, then, first see whether, since Truth and true are two words, it appears to you that they stand for two things or only for one?

A.   For two things, it seems to me. Thus, Chastity is one thing, the chaste another: and so of many others. I believe, therefore, Truth is one thing, and that which is said to be true another thing.

R.   And which of them do you consider the more excellent?

A.   Truth, in my judgment: for as Chastity is not the offspring of the chaste, but the chaste of Chastity, so, if anything be true it is true by reason of Truth.

28. R.   When a chaste person dies do you consider that Chastity dies also?

A.   Not at all.

R.   When, therefore, that which is true perishes, Truth does not perish.

A.   But how does anything true perish? I do not see.

R.   I am surprised that you ask that question, for do we not see constantly a thousand things perish before our eyes? Or do you, perhaps, consider this tree to be a tree, but not a true tree? Or not capable of perishing? For, although you do not believe in the senses, and may reply that you are not sure whether the tree exists or not, you will, nevertheless, not, I think, deny that, if it be a tree, it is a true tree; for this judgment is a matter not of sense, but of intelligence; for if it be a false tree it is not a tree, but if it be a tree it is of necessity a true tree.

A.   I concede this.

R.   And how of this also; do you not concede a tree to be of that class of things which are born and die?

A.   I cannot deny it.

R.   It is, then, concluded that a true thing may perish?

A.   I do not deny it.

R.   And, further, does it not appear that, though true things die, Truth does not die: just as, though the chaste person dies, Chastity does not die?

A.   I now concede this also, and eagerly await the outcome of your efforts.

R.   Pay attention, then.

A.   I am all attention.

29. R.   Does this proposition: — whatever is, is, of necessity, somewhere, seem true to you?

A.   Nothing so wins my consent.

R.   And do you admit that Truth is?

A.   I do.

R.   We must, then, of necessity inquire where she may be. She is not in some portion of space, unless you, perhaps, think that something else beside a body can occupy space, or that Truth is a body.

A.   I think neither of these things.

R.   Where, then, do you believe her to be? For we have agreed that what is, cannot be nowhere.

A.   If I knew where she were, I would not be likely to continue my researches.

R.   Are you, then, at least, able to conceive where she may be?

A.   If you suggest it, I may be able.

R.   She certainly is not in mortal things. For whatever is cannot survive in anything, if the thing in which it is does not survive. Also, it was, a little time ago, conceded that Truth remains, though true things pass away. Therefore Truth is not in mortal things. But Truth is, and is not nowhere. Therefore there are things immortal. But nothing is true in which Truth is not, and it therefore follows that nothing is, unless it be immortal: and every false tree is not a tree, and false wood is not wood, and false silver is not silver, and anything whatever which is false, is not. But everything which is not true, is false: therefore nothing can be rightly said to be except the immortal.

Now review this line of reasoning carefully, lest it should appear that some of your concessions ought not to have been made. If, however, it is valid, we have accomplished almost our entire undertaking, as will perhaps be better seen in a following book.

A.   I am grateful and give you thanks; and in the silence *Endnote 051* I will diligently and cautiously review these things with myself, and with you, provided no shadows reappear, causing me pleasure, as I so vehemently dread.

R.   Have constant faith in God, and commit your whole self to His care so far as you can! Refuse to be or to will as of your own power, and openly confess yourself to be a servant of this most merciful and gracious God; for so He will not forbear to uplift you to Himself, and will permit nothing save what is for your good to happen, even though you know it not!

A.   I hear, I believe, and I obey, so far as I have the power, and — unless you require something else of me — with all my soul I pray that I may have more and more power!

R.   And meanwhile, all is well. You will do hereafter whatever He Himself, having been seen, will instruct you.

BOOK II

I

1. A. Our work has been interrupted long enough. Love is impatient and unless to her is given what is loved, grief has no limit. Wherefore let us set about this second book.

R. Let us do so at once.

A. And let us believe that God will be with us!

R. Let us truly believe this, if that, indeed, be within our power.

A. Our power is Himself.

R. Pray then as briefly and concisely as you can.

A. God, always the same, let me know myself, let me know Thee! The prayer *Endnote 052* is made.

R. You, who desire to know yourself, do you know that you are?

A. I do. *Endnote 053*

R. How do you know this?

A. I do not know.

R. Do you feel yourself to be simple or complex?

A. I do not know.

R. Do you know yourself to be self-moved?

A. I do not.

R. Do you know that you think?

A. I do.

R. Is it then true that you think?

A. It is true. *Endnote 054*

R. Do you know yourself to be immortal? *Endnote 055*

A. I do not. *Endnote 056*

R. Which, among all these things of which you have declared yourself ignorant, would you choose to know first?

A. If I be immortal.

R. You love then to live?

A. I confess it.

R. Would it be enough if you should have learned that you were immortal?

A. It would, indeed, be much, but, for me, too little.

R. But this too little, how much joy will it cause you?

A. Very much joy.

R. Would you then weep for anything at all?

A. For nothing at all.

R. What if that immortal life were found to be such that it were permitted you to know there no more than you had known here, would you restrain your tears?

A. Nay, I would weep my life away!

R. You love, then, to live, not for the sake of living, but for the sake of knowing.

A. I grant the inference.

R. But suppose that this very knowledge should cause you misery?

A. That, indeed, I can believe in no case possible: but if it be, then no man can be happy. For now I am miserable from no cause save that of my ignorance, and if knowledge also shall cause me misery, then misery is eternal.

R. I now perceive the sum of your desires. For, believing that no man is made unhappy by knowledge, you argue that intelligence effects happiness: no man is happy if not living,

38

and no man lives who is not: you wish to be, to live, to know, but to be in order to live, and to live in order to know: now you know that you are, you know that you live, you know that you know. But whether all these things will continue forever; or whether no one of them will continue forever: whether some will survive and others will perish; or, in case all survive, whether they may become more and more, or must become less and less, this it is which you desire to know.

A.   So it is.

R.   And now, if we shall have proved that we are to live forever, it follows that we shall be forever.

A.   That follows.

R.   It will remain then to inquire concerning knowing.

II

2. A.   I perceive a very clear and concise order.

R.   At present, let the order be that you reply to my questions with caution and conviction.

A.   I am agreed.

R.   If this world shall continue forever, is it true that this world is to continue forever?

A.   Who doubts this?

R.   And if it is not to continue, is it not likewise true that it is not to continue?

A.   I do not contradict.

R.   And, when it shall have perished, if it is to perish, will it not then be true that the world has perished? For as long as it is true that the world has not passed away, it has not passed away: therefore the proposition that the world has passed away contradicts the proposition that the world has not passed away.

A.   This, too, I concede.

R.   And what about this? Does it seem to you that anything can be true and Truth not be?

A.   By no means.

R.   Therefore Truth will still be, even though the world should cease to be?

A.   I cannot deny it.

R.   What if Truth itself should perish, would it not be true that Truth had perished?

A.   And who denies that?

R.   But it cannot be true if Truth is not?

A.   That I have conceded, a little way back.

R.   Truth can, then, in no way perish?

A.   Nothing can be more true than this deduction; go on then, as you have begun.

Endnote 057

III

3. R.   I would like to have you now tell me whether it appears to you that the soul or the body has consciousness? *Endnote 058*

A.   It seems to me that it is the soul.

R.   And does it seem to you that the Intellect belongs to the soul?

A.   It seems so, unquestionably.

R.   To the soul alone, or to something beside?

A.   I see nothing else except the soul, unless it be God, which I can suppose the habitation of Intellect.

R.   Let us look into this. What would you think if some one should tell you that yonder wall was not a wall, but was a tree?

A.   Either that his senses or mine were in error; or that he had called a wall by that name.

R.   How if it had to you the appearance of a wall, and to him that of a tree: might not each be true?

A.   Not at all, for one and the same thing cannot be both a tree and a wall; and however it might appear to each of us separately as separate things, one of us must, of necessity, suffer a false conception.

R.   And how if it be neither tree nor wall, and both are deceived?

A.   That, of course, might be.

R.   This one point then, you overlooked above.

A.   I admit it.

R.   How if you both realized it to be something other than it appeared to you to be, would you be deceived, in that case?

A.   No.

R.   A thing can, then, have a false appearance to a person, and yet he will not be deceived by it?

A.   It can.

R.   It must, then, be granted that it is not he who sees false things who is deceived, but he only who assents to the false as true?

A.   Granted without doubt.

R.   What about the false itself — wherefore is the false, false?

A.   Because it appears to be other than it actually is.

R.   If, then, there are no persons to whom a thing appears, there is nothing false?

A.   That follows.

R.   Falsity, then, is not in things but in sense; and he who does not accept the false as true is not deceived: and if, when sense is deceived, we are not deceived, it must be granted that sense is one thing and we another.

A.   I have nothing to say in contradiction.

R.   But suppose the soul is deceived: would you venture, in this case, to declare that you are not deceived?

A.   By what possibility could I venture that far?

R.   But no sense without soul, and no falsity without sense. The soul, therefore, either operates or co-operates with falsity.

A.   What has preceded compels this conclusion.

4. R.   Tell me now if it seems to you possible that sometime falsity may not be. *Endnote 059*

A.   How could that seem possible to me when the difficulty of finding out Truth is so great that it seems more absurd to say that falsity may cease to exist than that Truth may?

R.   Do you think that he who does not live can have consciousness?

A.   That cannot be.

R.   Then it is established that the soul lives forever.

A.   You thrust joy upon me too precipitately; step by step, I beg!

R.   And yet, if the above concessions are correct, I see nothing to be in doubt concerning this matter.

A.   But I insist it is too soon. For I shall be more easily persuaded that I have made premature   concessions, than that I am already assured of the soul's immortality. Nevertheless, develop your argument, and let me see how you arrive at your conclusion.

R.   You have declared that falsity cannot fail to exist, and that it exists because of sense: sense, therefore, cannot cease to be. But there is no sense without soul. The soul is, therefore, everlasting. Nor can there be consciousness without life. The soul, therefore, lives forever.

IV

5. A.   O leaden dagger! For if I concede to you that the world could not exist apart from man, you are able to conclude that man is immortal, and that both he and the world are everlasting!

R.   You watch well! Nevertheless we have established no small matter in this — that the world of sense cannot exist apart from the soul, unless, perchance, there shall sometime be no falsity in the nature of things.

A.   I admit that to be the consequence. But I think we should now deliberate more amply as to the stability of our former concessions. For I see that no little progress has been made toward the soul's immortality.

R.   Have you sufficiently considered whether you may not have granted something too hastily?

A.   Quite sufficiently, and I see no lack of caution anywhere.

R.   It is then established that the nature of things cannot exist apart from a living soul?

A.   Established to this extent — that souls may succeed each other, those born succeeding those which die.

R.   And if falsity might be eliminated from the nature of things, might it not then come to pass, that all things would be true?

A.   That, I see, follows.

R.   Tell me why this wall seems to you to be true?

A.   Because I am not deceived by its appearance.

R.   Because it is in fact what it seems to be?

A.   Exactly.

R.   If, then, a thing is false from the fact that it appears other than it is, and true from the fact that it is as it appears, then the observer being removed there is nothing either true or false; but, if the falsity is removed from the nature of things, then all things are true. Nor can anything appear except to a living soul. The soul remains, therefore, in the framework of things, whether falsity can or cannot be eliminated.

A.   I see that our former inference is now made more solid: but we have made no real gain. For, not the less, does that which very much disturbs me remain; namely, that the world is never without souls, because since birth follows death, they are always here, not because of their immortality, but because of their succession.

6. R.   Does it seem to you that material things, that is, those appreciable by sense, can be wholly apprehended by the Intellect?

A.   It does not.

R.   What then? Does it seem to you that God makes use of senses for the cognition of things?

A.   I dare affirm nothing rashly concerning this point, but so far as I am permitted to conjecture, God in no way makes use of senses. *Endnote 060*

R.   We conclude then that consciousness is possible only to the soul.

A.   Tentatively, and so far as probability permits.

R.   How then? Do you grant that this wall, if not a true wall, is not a wall?

A.   I grant nothing more willingly.

R.   And that anything, if not a true body, is not a body?

A.   That also I admit.

R.   Therefore if nothing is true unless it be as it seems: nor can any sensible object have a seeming except to the senses: nor can anything except the soul have consciousness: nor any body be, unless it be a true body; it follows that unless the soul shall have been, the body cannot be.

A.   You urge me on so swiftly that what I might oppose, I cannot grasp. *Endnote 061*

V

7. R.   Attend even more diligently!

A.   Behold me here!

R.   This stone certainly is: and it is as such true if it is not in reality other than it seems: and if it is not true it does not exist: and it can have no seeming except to the senses.

A.   Even so.

R.   There are, then, no stones in the unseen bowels of the earth, nor anywhere where there are not those who can be conscious of them; nor, unless we shall behold it, can that stone be: and when we have gone elsewhere, it must cease to be, if no other human being remains to look at it: nor can coffers, however well filled, and securely closed, contain anything: nor can yonder wood be wood, except on its surface, since any body, not transparent to its depths, escapes every sense, and must, perforce, be considered non-existent. For if it were, it would be true: but anything is true only because it is as it appears: and this does not appear: therefore it is not true: or have you an answer to all this?

A.   I see that this is the outcome of those concessions of mine, but it is so absurd that I shall be more ready to recant whatever of them you choose, than to grant it to be true.

R.   I have no objection. See to it, then, which you prefer to declare: that bodies can appear independent of sense: or that consciousness can exist independent of soul: or that a stone or anything else can be and not be true: or that the true itself must be otherwise defined.

A.   Let us, I pray, consider this last alternative.

8. R.   Define, then, the true.

A.   That is true which actually is as it appears to the observer, if he can and will observe.

R.   That, therefore, which cannot be observed by some human being will not be true? Wherefore, if that be false which appears other than it really is, suppose this appears to one observer to be a stone and to another to be wood — shall the same thing be both false and true?

A.   That does not concern me so much as does the former proposition — that if a thing cannot be observed, it must follow that it cannot be true. I do not so much care that the same thing is at the same time both true and false: for, as a matter of fact, I observe that a certain thing, being compared with different things, may be both small and large, and thus it comes about that nothing is absolutely small or large, since these designations are simply relative.

R.   But, if you declare that nothing is true in itself, do you not fear lest it shall follow that nothing can be in itself? For, for the same reason that this is wood, it is also true wood. Nor is it a possible thing that in itself absolutely, that is, without an observer, it can be wood, and not be true wood.

A.   Therefore I declare and define thus, — nor do I fear that my definition shall be disproved because of brevity, — that seems to me to be true which is. *Endnote 062*

R.   Then nothing can be false, since whatever is, is true.

A.   You have driven me into close quarters, nor do I, immediately, find an answer. It has come to this, that while I am unwilling to be taught in any way except by these questions, I, nevertheless, fear to be longer questioned.

VI

9. R.   God, to whom we have committed ourselves, has, without doubt, this work in hand, and will deliver us from our straits, if only we believe, and pray to Him with all the heart.

A.   Nothing would I, at this pass, do more gladly, for never have I been involved in such pitchy darkness. *Endnote 063* O God, our Father, who dost exhort us to pray, and dost grant what we ask, if so be that when we pray to Thee we are better and live better; listen to me, groping amid these shadows, and stretch out to me Thy right hand! Hold Thy Light before me! Call me back from wandering! Under Thy guidance, let me return to myself, let me return to Thee! Amen!

R.   Concentrate your attention now as much as is possible and listen most watchfully!

A.   Speak, I implore, if anything is borne in upon you, lest we perish!

R.   Concentrate your attention!

A.   Behold me, I am all attention!

10. R.   Let us then first ventilate the truth about this question — what is Falsity?

A.   I wonder if it shall be found to be anything else than that which is not as it seems.

R.   Be more attentive, while we first cross-examine the senses themselves. Now it is certain that which the eyes behold is not pronounced false unless it possess some likeness to the true. For example, the man we see in a dream is not a true man, but a false, by the very fact that he bears some resemblance to the true. For, who, having seen in his dream a dog, could rightly say that he dreamed of a man? The dog, also, is false, because he is like a true one.

A.   It is as you say.

R.   And when a person, wide-awake, takes a horse for a man, is he not deceived by this very fact, that it appears to him in some similitude of a man? For if to him it appears like nothing but a horse, it is not possible that he should think he sees a man.

A.   I agree to this without reserve.

R.   In the same manner, we call the picture of a tree a false tree, the face reflected from a mirror a false face, the apparent motion of towers to those sailing past them, a false motion, the apparent break of the oak under water a false break, from no other reason than because they are similar to the true.

A.   I admit it.

R.   And we are, likewise, deceived by the similarity in twins, and in eggs, and in the impressions of a seal ring, and in other such things.

A.   I follow and wholly agree with you.

R.   That similitude of things, which obtains by the sense of sight, is, therefore, the mother of Falsity.

A.   I cannot deny it.

11. R.   Now this whole forest of facts can, if I mistake not, be divided into two classes: the one containing things equal, the other things unequal: equals, when, for instance, we say this is like that as that is like this, as is said in the case of twins, and of the impressions of a seal ring: unequals, when the inferior is said to be like the superior. For who, looking into a mirror, could possibly declare that he resembled his own reflected image, and not rather that it resembled him? And this class subdivides again into one which contains those cases which have a purely mental origin and one which contains those brought about by sense. Again, those which are experienced by the mind are twofold: those induced by the senses, as in the

fictitious motion of the towers: or by itself from that which it received from the senses, as in the visions of those dreaming and perhaps, also, of the insane. Moreover those objects of the sense of sight which appear to us as if really the things they look like, are produced and fashioned, some by nature, some by living beings. Nature produces these inferior similitudes either by reproduction or representation: by reproduction, as when children are born resembling their parents, by representation, as in the case of every sort of reflector; for, although men make nearly all mirrors, they do not make the images reflected from them.

Now the productions of living beings consist of pictures and delineations of every sort whatever, in which class may be included, also, those apparitions, if such there be, produced by spirits. The shadows of substances, also, may properly have a place in this category: for, since they are similitudes of bodies, and in a sense false bodies, they cannot be denied a place among those things belonging to the realm of vision, as produced by nature from reflection. For every body turned to the sun reflects light, and on the opposite side casts a shadow. Or does something contradictory occur to you?

A. Nothing indeed: but I wait with impatience to see whither these things tend.

12. R. It is now our duty to patiently persevere until the other senses have given their testimony to our proposition that Falsity has its seat in similitude to the true. For from the sense of hearing almost as many kinds of similitude are to be observed; as when, hearing the voice, but not seeing the person, we think it is that of one whose voice it is similar to: and, among these inferior similitudes, echo, the ringing in the ears, and the imitation in clocks of the notes of the blackbird or the crow, or those sounds which the sleeping and the insane seem to themselves to hear, are all witnesses. And it is incredible how much false notes, as musicians *Endnote 064* call them, witness to this truth, as will be seen hereafter; although it suffices for the present, that they are not lacking in similitude to those which are called true. Do you follow me?

A. Most willingly, for I find no difficulty in understanding.

R. Well, then, not to lose time; does it seem to you that one lily is distinguishable from another by its perfume? The thyme-honey of one hive from the thyme-honey of another by its taste? The softness of the swan's plumage from that of the goose by its touch?

A. It does not.

R. And how, when in dreams we seem to taste or touch or smell such things, are we not deceived in these imaginations by a similitude inferior in proportion to its nothingness?

A. You speak truly.

R. It appears, then, that we are deceived in all our senses by some seductive similitude — whether of things equal or things inferior: or, if not actually deceived, as suspending consent and discriminating differences, we nevertheless designate as false those things which we find similar to the true.

A. I cannot doubt it.

VII

13. R.   Now give attention, as we again briefly review the same thing, so that this which we endeavor to show may become yet more obvious.

A.   I hear: say what you will, for I have made up my mind, once for all, to submit to this roundabout route without impatience, because of my great hope of arriving at the goal toward which I feel that we are tending.

R.   You do well. But now consider whether it seems to you that when we see a number of similar eggs, we can say, with truth, that any one of them is false?

A.   By no means: for, if all are eggs, all are true eggs.

R.   And how is it in the case of an image reflected from a mirror? By what signs do we apprehend it to be false?

A.   Because, of course, it cannot be grasped, does not give forth sound, has not power to move itself, does not live, and we apprehend it also by other innumerable things which it would be tiresome to elaborate.

R.   I see that you are unwilling to delay, and something must be yielded to your impatience. Not to repeat, then, each detail, — suppose those men whom we see in dreams as if living and speaking could be held captive by us when waking, and found to be no different themselves from those whom wide-awake and in our senses we see and talk with — could we call them false?

A.   How could they possibly be so called?

R.   If, then, they were true by reason of their appearing perfectly similar to the true, so that nothing whatever differentiates them from the true: and false by reason of corresponding or other differences, must it not be admitted also that similitude is the mother of Truth and dissimilitude of Falsity? *Endnote 065*

A.   I have nothing to answer, and am ashamed of my former so hasty assent.

14. R.   It is absurd for you to be ashamed, for we have provided for such an event by our choice of this method of discussion, which, because we speak to ourselves alone, I wish to have designated and written down as Soliloquies, — certainly a new, and perhaps, unattractive name, but quite suitable to the matter under discussion. For, while Truth cannot be better investigated than by question and answer, scarce a person can be found who is not mortified at being vanquished in argument, and from this fact it almost invariably happens that, when the debate is well under way, some explosion of perversity bursts out resulting in wounded feelings, often concealed, but sometimes apparent; so that I think it tends most to peace and is best suited to the search after Truth *Endnote 066* that, God helping, I myself reply to questions put by myself. Therefore there is no need that we should fear to turn back and reconsider, if at any time from lack of deliberation you should have tangled yourself up; for otherwise there is no way out.

VIII

15. A.   Well said! but I do not see clearly that I have made any incorrect concession, unless in fact it be in having declared that to be false, which possesses some similitude to the true: as nothing else occurs to me which clearly deserves to be called false. Yet, on the other hand, I am forced to admit that those things designated as false are so called by reason of that in which they are unlike the true: and so it turns out that dissimilitude itself is also the cause of falsity: therefore I am perplexed, for I cannot easily conceive how a thing can be the result of antagonistic causes.

R.   But how if this be the single such case, and is thus unique? Or, do you not know that, passing in review the innumerable species of animals, the crocodile is the only one to move his upper jaw in masticating? *Endnote 067* And that it is notorious that scarcely anything can be found which is so like another in every detail, that somedetail is not discovered in which it is unlike?

A.   I do indeed perceive this. But when I realize that what we call false possesses both likeness and unlikeness to the true, I cannot decide from which of the two this designation of false is better deserved. For if I say it is from that by which it differs, nothing will remain which cannot be called false: for, among those things admitted to be true, there is nothing which is not in some detail, unlike everything else. If, on the other hand, I say it is from that in which they resemble that things deserve the name of false, not only will those eggs which are true, in that they are similar, protest, but also I shall not escape him who would force me to admit that all things are false, since I cannot deny that all things are, in some respect, similar to each other. But, supposing I do not fear to answer him that likeness and unlikeness co-operate at the same time to bring it about that a thing may correctly be called false, what refuge from this dilemma will you provide? I shall be forced to allow that all things are false, since, as I have just said above, all things are found to be in some respects alike, in others unlike. My sole alternative would be to say that the false is nothing else than that which appears otherwise than it actually is, did I not fear those many monsters of which I was thinking I had long ago steered clear. For, once more, I am suddenly whirled giddily around in order that I may announce that the true is that which appears what it actually is. It next transpires that, without a cognizer, nothing can be true, and I am menaced with shipwreck upon those hidden reefs, which are true reefs, though without a cognizer. And if I say that the true is that which is, it must follow, in spite of all contradiction, that no place is left for the false. And so all my unrest returns, and I do not see that I have gained anything by so much patience with your delays.

IX

16. R.   Take heed, rather! For I will not at all harbor the suggestion that we have sought divine aid in vain: *Endnote 068* I see, indeed, by our many experiments in all these things, that nothing remains which can justly be called false, save that which feigns to be what it is not, or, in general, that which tends to be and is not. Of the former type of false things are those which are either actually misleading or those which are simply fictitious. Of the misleading it may be said truly that it has a certain appetite for deceiving, which cannot be conceived to exist apart from soul, and results, on the one hand, from reason, on the other from nature. But the fictitious I call that which is produced by makers of fiction: these differ from the misleading in this, that every misleader has a desire to deceive: while not every fiction-maker has. For mimes and comedies and many poems are full of fictions for the purpose rather of pleasing than of deceiving: and almost all who make jests deal in fictions. But he is rightly called a misleader, or misleading, whose business it is that everybody should be deceived. Others, however, who have no purpose to deceive in what they do, but do, nevertheless, manufacture things, are, so far, falsifiers: or, if not actually that, yet, no man doubts that they deserve the name of fiction-makers. Or have you something to say in contradiction?

17. A.   Proceed, I beg. For now you are, perhaps, beginning to teach concerning falsity, not falsely. But I am expecting to hear of what sort that may be of which you say: — It tends to be and is not.

R.   And why not? For they are those of which we have taken note in many things above. For does not your image in the mirror seem to you as if it willed to be your very self, but to be false for the reason that it is not?

A.   It seems so indeed.

R.   And every picture, every representation of every sort, everything among the works of art of that class, do they not strive, as it were, to be after the likeness of that in imitation of which they are made?

A.   I am positively convinced of this.

R.   And you now concede, I suppose, that those things by which dreamers or the insane are deceived are of this sort?

A.   None more so: for none so tend toward reality and those things which the waking and sane see. They are, nevertheless, false, in that they tend toward being and cannot attain to it.

R.   And what now of the apparent motion of the towers? — of the oar bent beneath the water? — of the shadows of bodies? Need I say more? For it is, as I think, evident that they should all come under the same classification.

A.   Most evident.

R.   I do not speak of the other senses: for there is no thoughtful man but has found that among those things which we experience in sensible matters, that is called false which tends to be and is not. *Endnote 069*

X

18. A.   You speak truly: but I wonder why it seems to you that poems and jests and other fictions should be excluded from this class?

R.   Because to will to be false is one thing, and to be unable to be true is another. Thus the works themselves of men, whether comedies or tragedies or mimes, and other things of that sort, we are able to classify along with the works of painters and sculptors. For a painted man cannot be so true, however much he approximates the appearance of a man, as are those things which are written in the books of the comic poets. For these neither will to be false, nor are they false by any appetite of their own: but by a certain necessity they carry out, as much as possible, the intention of their author. Thus Roscius, by his own will, was, upon the stage, a false Hecuba: though by nature he was a true man, but a true tragedian by that very will by which he filled the rôle as such, and a false Priam, in that he was simulating Priam though not he himself. And from this comes to pass a certain marvel, which, however, no man doubts to be an actual fact.

A.   What is that?

R.   What do you suppose, except that all these things are true in some respects from the fact that they are false in others, and that their proper rôles can be produced by them only because they are false to others? Wherefore if they desist from these falsities, they can by no means achieve that which they wish and are in duty bound to do. For by what possibility could he whom I have cited be a true tragedian if he were unwilling to be a false Andromache, a false Hector, a false Hercules, and countless others. Or whence would a picture of a horse be a true picture, if it were not a false horse? And whence is that reflection from the mirror a true reflection if it be not a false man? And why, since, in order that certain things may be true in something, they must be false in something, do we so greatly fear falsities and so eagerly hunger after truth?

A.   I do not know and I much wonder, except it be that I see these examples to be in nothing worthy of emulation. *Endnote 070* For, in order to be true in our own individual characters, we ought not to become false, by imitating and taking the rôle of others, as do actors, and the reflections from mirrors, and Myron's brazen cow: but to seek the true, which is not double-faced, and self-contradictory, nor in order that it may be true on one side, false on the other.

R.   Great and divine things are these which you demand. And if we shall have found them, shall it not be confessed that Truth itself, after which everything which is in any way true is discriminated and named, has been, as it were, created and breathed into life by what has preceded?

A.   I do not withhold my assent.

XI

19. R.   Does it seem to you that the science of disputation is a true science or a false?
Endnote 071

A.   Who doubts its truth? But grammar is also a true science.

R.   As true?

A.   I do not see that anything is truer than the true.

R.   That certainly which has in it nothing of false: investigating this, a little way back, you were offended that some things I know not how, could not be true, save on condition that they were also false. Do you not, then, know that things both fabulous and obviously false are within the province of grammar?

A.   I am, indeed, not ignorant of that fact: but, as I judge, it is not through grammar they are shown to be of whatever sort they are. A fable is, in fact, a fictitious composition for the purpose of entertainment or utility. The science of grammar is also the custodian and disciplinarian of spoken language, and is compelled, by necessity of its vocation, to collect all productions, oral or written, in literature, not making them false, but taking them in charge and teaching what is true and reasonable concerning them.

R.   Right and sound, though it is not at present my concern whether these things be correctly defined and discriminated: but I ask this: — Whether it is grammar or science of disputation which truly so demonstrates all this?

A.   I do not deny that force and skill in defining, by which I have just now tried to distinguish these things, belong to the art of the disputant.

20. R.   How about grammar itself? If true, is it not true by that by which it is a science? The word science is derived from the verb to learn: — now no man learns and retains what he learns, who cannot be said to know: and no man knows the false: every science, therefore, is true.

A.   I do not see that anything in this little argument is incautiously reasoned. But I am disturbed lest some one will conclude that those fables even are true, since we both learn and remember them.

R.   Was our master ever unwilling that we should both know and believe these fables which he was accustomed to teach?

A.   On the contrary, he was wont to insist with vehemence *Endnote 072* that we should know them.

R.   Did he ever insist that we should believe that Daedalus flew?

A.   That, indeed, never. But if we did not learn the fable itself perfectly, he would so conduct himself that we could scarcely keep anything in our hands.

R.   Do you then deny that it is true that such a fable exists, and that Daedalus is so reported everywhere?

A.   I do not deny that that is true.

R.   You do not deny, then, that when you learned that, you learned a true thing? For, if it be true that Daedalus flew, and the boys received and recited it as fable and a fiction: they would, by that, have retained something false; because those things which they recited were true. And so what we were marvelling at before comes to pass: that unless it be false that Daedalus flew, the fable concerning the flight of Daedalus cannot be a true fable.

A.   I grasp that, at last, but wait to see how we are going to profit by it.

R.   How except that it is not a false reasoning by which we infer that a science cannot be a science, unless it teach true things.

A.   And how is that to the point?

R.   Because I wish you to tell me what makes grammar a science. For from whence it is true, from thence it is a science.

A.   I do not know how to answer you.

R.   Do you consider that if there were in it nothing of definition, distinction or classification, it could, in any sense, be called a science?

A.   I see now what you mean to say: nor does there occur to me anything in the guise of any sort of science, in which there are not definitions, classifications, and argumentations, so that any proposition may be analyzed, each thing relevant to it being relegated without confusion to its proper place, nothing belonging to it omitted, nothing alien admitted, all things working together to make that very whole which is by that given the name of science.

R.   And that very whole, therefore, by which it is called true.

A.   I see that that follows.

21. R.   Now tell me what science contains the principles of definition, classification and distribution?

A.   I have already said, above, that they are contained in the laws governing the science of disputation.

R.   Grammar, then, is constituted by that same art, which you have before defended from the charge of falsity, both a science and true. And this I am permitted to conclude, not alone of grammar, but of absolutely all sciences. For you have said, and said truly, that no science occurs to you in which the law of definition and of distribution is not the very thing which constitutes it a science. And if, by the same reason that they are sciences, they are true, can any one deny that that through which they are all true sciences is Truth itself?

A.   I am certainly very near agreeing to this. But it disturbs me that we reckon also among all these sciences that principle of debate itself. Whereas, I should consider that it is rather Truth itself by which that principle is true.

R.   Altogether watchful and excellent! But you do not, I suppose, deny that a science is true from that by which it is a science?

A.   It is indeed because of that, that I am disturbed. For I have adverted to it as itself a science, and on that account have declared it to be true.

R.   How then? Do you consider that it could be a science otherwise, except as in it all things are defined and classified?

A.   I have nothing to say.

R.   But if this is its province, it is through itself proved a true science. Who, then, would deem it strange if this, through which all things are true, should in itself and through itself be true Truth?

A.   Nothing whatever hinders me now from advancing to that opinion. *Endnote 073*

XII

22. R.   Attend, then, to the few things which remain.

A.   If what you have to offer be in such wise as I can comprehend, I will freely assent.

R.   We do not fail to perceive that a thing is said to be in something in two ways. In the one way it can be disunited and be separate, and in another place, as this wood in that place, or as the sun in the east. In another way a thing is so in its subject that separation from it is impossible, as is the form and quality in the wood, or as is light in the sun, or heat in fire, or knowledge in the mind, and other things similarly. Or do you see it to be otherwise?

A.   All this is most familiar to me, and since early youth *Endnote 074* has been most studiously observed and known. Wherefore if interrogated concerning it, I can assent without hesitation.

R.   Do you, then, concede that what is inseparable from its subject cannot survive if the subject dies?

A.   That, too, I see, of necessity, follows. For even when the subject abides, it is possible that what is in the subject may not abide, as whoever diligently considers the matter knows. Thus, the color of my body may, either by reason of age or of illness, change, while the body is yet living. And this obtains, not of all things equally, but of those things which, while they are not themselves subjects, but only in the subject, yet co-exist with it. For that wall which we see to be of a certain color, need not, in order that it be a wall, be of that color; for if, by some chance, it becomes white or black or some other color, it, nevertheless, remains a wall and is so called. But if fire lack heat, it will not truly be fire at all: nor can we call snow snow, unless it be white.

XIII

23. That, however, which you have asked — whether that which is in the subject remains, the subject having perished — who could allow, or to whom would it seem to be possible? For it is monstrous and most alien to the truth that that which, unless it were in the subject, could not possibly exist, could still exist even when the subject does not.

R.   That, then, which we were seeking is found.

A.   What do you say?

R.   What you hear.

A.   Is it, then, already established beyond question that the soul is immortal?

R.   If what you have conceded is true, wholly beyond question. Unless you may say that the mind, even though it may die, is still the mind?

A.   Never, indeed, will I say that: but I do say that if it can perish, by that very fact it is not the mind. Nor will I retract this opinion because great philosophers *Endnote 075* have declared that it cannot admit death within its essence, but that, wherever it goes, it is still instinct with life. For, although light illumines any place into which it can enter, and, by reason of that famous law of contraries, cannot admit darkness into itself, yet, let it be extinguished and that same place, the light having been put out, becomes dark. And so that which is antagonistic to darkness, nor can in any way admit it into its own essence, may yet, by dying, give place to it, as it could have done, indeed, by departing. And so, I fear lest it may be that death may befall the body as darkness a place, by the soul, like a light, sometime departing thence, but sometimes being extinguished in the body. And as now there can be no security against the death of the body, yet that kind of death is to be preferred by which the soul is led forth, unharmed, and conducted to a place (if such place there be) where it cannot be put out. But if this may not be, and if the soul is kindled, like a flame, within the every essence of the body, nor can elsewhere endure, then every kind of death is extinction of the life of the body and the soul alike. And that mode of life should be chosen, so far as is permitted man to choose, in which that which does live may live in safety and tranquillity, though I know not, if the soul dies, how that is possible. Oh, very happy they who, whether by themselves, or by whatever cause, are persuaded that death, even though the soul perish, is not to be feared! *Endnote 076* But no reasoning, no books have, so far, persuaded miserable me.

24. R.   Do not lament! The human soul is immortal.

A.   How is it proven?

R.   By those things which you have already, with very great caution, conceded.

A.   I do not, indeed, recall anything which, replying to you, I have granted with any small degree of vigilance. But now I beg you bring them all together to that one conclusion. I do not, for the present, wish you to question me, but let us see by what great circumlocution we have come hither. For if you are about to briefly enumerate the things which I have already conceded, to what end would my repetition of them be desired? Or why should you wantonly inflict upon me the postponement of joy, if, indeed, we have perchance accomplished anything of good?

R.   I see and I will do what you desire, but pay most diligent attention.

A.   Here I am, speak now: why torture me to death?

R.   If everything which is in the subject persists forever, the subject itself must, of necessity, persist forever. And every science is in the mind as subject. It is, then, a necessary fact that the mind continues forever, if science continues forever. But science is Truth, and, as Reason has convinced you at the beginning of this book, Truth continues forever. The mind, therefore, abides; nor can it be called mortal. He alone, therefore, without absurdity denies that the mind is undying, who proves any of the foregoing conclusions to be untrue.

XIV

25. A.   I would give myself up to joy forthwith, except that two causes restrain me. For, first, I am disturbed that we have made use of so much circumlocution, following I know not what chain of reasoning, when, as is now shown, the whole matter at which we have been laboring could have been so briefly demonstrated. Wherefore it makes me anxious that our discourse has gone so roundabout as if for some insidious purpose. And, next, I do not see how knowledge can be inbred in the mind's essence, when so few are well versed in it, especially in that science of disputation: for, surely, if any one may have become familiar with it, he yet must have been, from infancy, and a long time thereafter, ignorant of it. Neither can we say that the minds of the unlearned are not minds, or that knowledge of which they are ignorant, is in them. For if that be extremely absurd, it remains either that Truth is not forever in the mind, or that that science is not the Truth.

26. R.   You see that not in vain has our reasoning pursued its way circuitously. For we have been seeking to find out what Truth is, though I see that we have not so far been able to discover it in this particular forest of facts whose by-ways have almost all been explored. But what are we to do? Shall we give up the undertaking and wait until, perchance, some other books may fall into our hands which shall satisfy this questioning? For I think many have been written before our age which we have not read; and, in order that we may not express opinions of that concerning which we are ignorant, we have within reach writings concerning this subject, both in prose and in verse, by men whose works are not unknown to us, and whose talents we know well, so that we cannot be without hope of finding that for which we are wishing in their books, especially when he is here before our eyes in whom we have recognized a revival in perfection of that eloquence which we had mourned as dead. _Endnote 077_ And will he who has, in his own writings, taught us the way of life, permit us to remain in ignorance of the nature of life?

A.   I do not think so indeed, and I hope much from thence: but I grieve that we do not succeed in disclosing to him, as we would like, either our attitude toward himself or toward wisdom. He, surely, would pity our thirst, and would overflow to us far more often than at present is the case. For he, because already convinced, is assured and at ease concerning the immortality of the soul: nor does he, perchance, know that there are those who have too long experienced the wretchedness of doubt, and whom, especially when they ask, it were cruel not to succor. _Endnote 078_

And there is another who knows full well, from long familiarity, our intense anxiety; but he is so far away, and we are so situated, that scarcely have we any opportunity of even so much as sending him a letter. In transalpine leisure he has, I believe, produced a poem by which the fear of death, exorcised, flees away, and that chill and stupor of the soul, unyielding as the ice of ages, is cast out. _Endnote 079_ But, in the meantime, while we wait for these helps to those things which are not in our power, is it not most shameful that our time should be thrown away, and the whole mind itself, from this wavering judgment, hang in suspense?

XV

27. Where is that God whom we have prayed and implored, not for riches, not for pleasures, not for high places and popular honors, but for an open way for us seeking our own soul and Himself? Does He thus, then, desert us or is He deserted by us? *Endnote 080*

R.   Most foreign to Himself is it that He should desert those who seek such things; and, therefore, it should be foreign to us to desert such a Leader. Wherefore, if you please, let us briefly review the reasoning by which it is concluded that Truth continues forever, and that the principle of disputation is Truth. For you have declared that those propositions are not firmly established, and that therefore we are not secure in our conclusions. Or shall we, instead, seek to know how it is that knowledge can dwell in an untrained mind, which we cannot refuse to call a mind, because untrained? For you seem to be troubled, so that it is needful to again debate those things which you had conceded.

A.   Nay, let us, first, discuss the former matter and afterwards we shall see what there may be of the latter. For thus, there will, I think, be an end of controversy.

R.   Let it be so then: but bring to it the utmost caution and concentration. For I observe that while you are listening, it comes about that, from your great anxiety to reach a conclusion, you are looking for it to present itself the next minute; and so you concede propositions which are put to you before they are thoroughly examined.

A.   Perhaps you are right, and I will do my best to overcome this infirmity. Begin, then, your questions, lest we lose time over superfluous matters.

28. R.   We have, as I recollect, concluded that Truth cannot perish, for the reason that should not only the whole world pass away but even Truth itself, it would still be true that the world and Truth had perished. But nothing can be true without Truth. In no sense, then, can Truth perish.

A.   I recognize these conclusions, and shall be very much astonished if they prove false.

R.   Let us, then, look into the other matter.

A.   Permit me, I beg, to reconsider yet a little lest I again retreat in disgrace.

R.   Shall it then not be true that Truth has perished? If it be not true, then it has not perished. If it be true, how can it be true, after Truth has perished, when now there is no Truth?

A.   Nothing now remains which I need further reconsider. Proceed, therefore, to the other matter. We will certainly do all in our power, so that learned and prudent men may read and correct any inadvertence which may be found; though I do not think that, either now or at any future time, anything can be said against this conclusion.

29. R.   Is, then, Truth called Truth from any other reason save that it is that by which any true thing is true?

A.   From no other thing.

R.   And is anything rightly called true except because it is not false?

A.   This, surely, it were madness to doubt.

R.   And is not the false that which approximates to the likeness of the true, yet is not that which it resembles?

A.   Nothing else, indeed, do I see which can so readily be called false. It is, nevertheless, customary to call that false which is very far from resembling the true.

R.   Who denies that? But even so it still holds, by some slight imitation to the true.

A.   How so? For when it is said that Medea flew with winged serpents yoked, on what side does that statement, forsooth, imitate the true, seeing it is nothing? [Endnote 081] For it is impossible that a thing which absolutely cannot be, can be imitated.

R.   You speak truly; but do you not observe that this which is absolutely nothing, cannot even be said to be false? For if false, it is; and if it is not, it is not false.

A.   May we not, then, say that this inconceivably monstrous thing about Medea is false?

R.   Certainly not: for if false, how is it monstrous?

A.   I see, then, a miracle! And so, forsooth, when I hear
"With mighty, winged snakes hitched to her car"
I call it not false?

R.   You do, obviously. For that which you declare false is.

A.   What is, I beg?

R.   That sentence which is enunciated by the verse.

A.   And how, pray, does that possess any imitation of the true?

R.   In its enunciation; which is such as it would be if Medea had actually done that thing. The false sentence imitates the true sentence in its structure. Which, if not credited, in that it imitates the true only in the manner of the telling, is so false that it does not even deceive. If it claims belief it must imitate credible truths.

A.   I now perceive that there is a vast difference between things which we simply repeat, and things by which we predicate something. Wherefore I now agree. For this alone — that we correctly call nothing false except it possess some imitation of a true thing — gave me pause. For who would not be justly ridiculed if he called that stone yonder false silver? But if he affirmed that stone to be silver, we say that he makes a false statement, that is, that he gives utterance to a false judgment. But we might, I think, without absurdity, call lead or zinc false silver because it imitates, as it were, that very thing: nor is our judgment about it false, but the thing itself about which the judgment is expressed.

XVI

30. R.   You understand well. But now observe whether we can appropriately call silver by the name of false lead.

A.   That does not please me.

R.   Why so?

A.   I do not know. I only perceive that it is violently against my will that it is so called.

R.   May it be, perhaps, because, if so called, silver being the superior, would seem to be dishonored? Whereas it is a sort of honor to lead to be called false silver.

A.   You have explained it exactly as I was wishing to. And so it is, I believe, that those who display themselves in the dress of women are held in law to be disreputable and incapacitated for witness-bearing, *Endnote 082* and I know not whether these are best called false women or false men. We may, at any rate, call them true actors and true outlaws. And if they sneak around, we may, since no one save by disgraceful repute gets such a name, call them true good-for-nothings.

R.   There will be another opportunity for the discussion of these things. For many things which, by popular esteem, seem to be shameful, can yet be shown to have their origin in an honest and laudable purpose. For example, it is a great question whether, for the purpose of obtaining the liberties of one's country, he who assumes the garb of a woman to the end of misleading the enemy, does not become all the more a man thereby; or whether a wise man, though persuaded that his life is, in some way, essential to human affairs, should, nevertheless, choose rather to die of cold than to be wrapped in the garments of a woman, no others being available. But, as we have said, we can look into this matter later on. For you must be aware how great a degree of discrimination is needed to decide how far such things may be carried without falling into inexcusable improprieties. But it suffices for the present, I think, that it now appears beyond doubt that nothing can be false save by some imitation of the true.

XVII

31. A. Pass on to what remains, for I am well persuaded of this.

R. I ask, then, whether, with the exception of those sciences by which we have been educated — among which the study of wisdom should itself be counted — we can find anything so true that, like the Achilles in the play, it must not be false on the one side in order that it may be true on the other?

A. It seems to me that there are many. For we do not, by any science, judge that stone yonder to be a stone, nor, in order that it may be a true stone, does it imitate something, and thus be called false. This one example being cited, you see innumerable others following on, which to those pondering the matter, occur spontaneously.

R. I see, of course. But do not all these seem to you to be comprised under the one name of body?

A. They would seem so if I held either that the inane were nothing, or that the soul itself ought to be included among corporeal things, or if I might believe that even God Himself is a body of some kind. All of these things, if they are, I do not see to be true or false, by imitation of anything else.

R. You are sending me a long way, but I will use such dispatch as is possible. For assuredly what you call the inane is one thing and Truth is another.

A. Far other. For what more inane than I, if I deem it to be inane, and thus hunger so greatly after the inane? For what but Truth do I desire to discover?

R. And so you do concede, perchance, that nothing is true unless made so by Truth?

A. That, long ago, was shown to be the case.

R. And do you doubt whether anything is inane except the inane itself, or certainly, whether a body is?

A. I do not at all doubt it.

R. I judge then that you believe Truth to be a sort of body.

A. By no means.

R. What is there in a body?

A. I do not know: it is not to the point, for I think you know that the inane, if there be inane, is more inane where no body is.

R. That is obviously a sound conclusion.

A. Why, then, do we delay?

R. Does it seem to you that Truth has caused the inane, or that anything can be true where Truth is not?

A. It does not.

R. The inane, then, cannot be true, for the reason that the inane cannot be the offspring of that which is not inane: and whatsoever is without Truth is, manifestly, not true; and, in short, what is called inane, is so called because it is nothing: how, therefore, can that be true which is nothing? Or how can that which is intrinsically nothing be at all?

A. Come, let us leave the inane to be inane!

XVIII

32. R.   What have you to say to the rest?

A.   What rest?

R.   That which you see me so concerned about. For God and the soul remain, which two if true, are so because the Truth is in them; but no man doubts concerning the immortality of God. Also, the mind is believed to be immortal, if Truth, which cannot perish, is really proved to be in it. Wherefore let us now examine the last point — whether the body may not be truly true, that is, not that Truth is in it, but a certain image, as it were, of Truth. For if in the body, which is quite certain to admit the perishable, we shall have found something true in such sort as in the sciences, then Truth will not be, necessarily, that science of disputation by which all sciences are true. For the body which does not seem to be formed by the principle of disputation, is true. If, in fact, the body is true, by reason of some sort of imitation, and yet, on that account, also, not absolutely true, there will still then be nothing, perhaps, to prevent that principle of disputation from being taught to be the very Truth itself.

A.   In the meantime, let us inquire concerning the body. For until this point shall have been settled, I see no end of the controversy.

R.   How do you know what God wills? Attend, therefore; for I judge that the body is contained in some sort of form and appearance, which it would not have if it were not a body: for if it had reality, it would be the mind. Or do you think otherwise?

A.   I agree in part; in part I hesitate. I concede that, unless it held to some conformation, a body could not exist. But how, if it held to a true conformation, it would be the mind — that I do not quite see.

R.   Do you, then, after all, recall nothing of the exordium of our first book concerning that geometry of yours?

A.   It is well that you have reminded me. I recall it immediately and most willingly.

R.   Are such figures as that science demonstrates found in bodies?

A.   On the contrary, it is incredible how inferior bodies are shown to be.

R.   Which, then, of the two, do you consider the true?

A.   Do not, I beg, consider that I need to be even questioned on that point. For who so blind of mind that he must not perceive that those things which geometry demonstrates dwell in that very Truth, or rather that Truth dwells in them? While embodied figures, while they seem as if tending toward these, possess I know not what imitation of Truth, and are, therefore, false. For now I see the whole matter which you were striving to make clear.

XIX

33. R.   Why need we now inquire further concerning the science of disputation? For whether the figures of geometry are in the Truth, or the Truth is in them, no man doubts, that they are contained in the soul, that is, in the intelligence. And thus Truth is, of necessity, forced to be in the mind. For if any science whatever is inseparable from the mind as subject, and if the Truth cannot die, why, I ask, do we — by I know not what familiarity with death — doubt concerning the everlasting life of the mind? Or do the line and rectangle and circle possess other features which they imitate in order that they may be true?

A.   By no means am I able to believe that, unless a line may be perhaps something other than length without breadth, or a circle something other than a curved line everywhere equally distant from the centre.

R.   Why, then, do we hesitate? Or are those things where Truth is not?

A.   May God avert such madness!

R.   Or is knowledge not in the mind?

A.   Who would say that?

R.   But it may, perhaps, be that, though the subject perish, that which is in the subject may survive?

A.   When shall I be persuaded of that?

R.   It remains, then, that Truth may perish.

A.   How can that be?

R.   The soul, then, is immortal. Believe now your own argument, believe the Truth! She cries aloud that she dwells within you, that she is immortal, that by no death whatsoever of the body can her throne be filched away from her. Turn away from your shadows! Turn back to yourself! Nothing of you is mortal, save your forgetfulness of your own immortality.

A.   I hear. I come to myself. I begin to remember! But I beg of you hasten that which remains, namely: how, in a mind untrained, since we cannot call it mortal, may science and Truth be understood to exist?

R.   That question, if you would thoroughly explore it, requires another volume. At the same time, I perceive that those things which we have investigated should be reviewed by you, for, if no one of those which you have conceded is in doubt, I consider that we have accomplished much, and may apply ourselves to what remains with no small degree of confidence.

XX

34. A.   It is as you say, and I willingly follow your instructions; but this much at least let me secure before you decree an end to this volume, namely, that you briefly indicate that which distinguishes between the true figure which is contained in the intelligence, and that which thought fashions for itself, which is called in Greek phantasy or phantasm. *Endnote 083*

R.   That which you demand can be seen only by one wholly pure, and you are, as yet, unprepared for this vision; nor do we toil through these many circuits for aught else save your disciplining, to the end that you may become fit to see this difference. Nevertheless I can briefly show you how it can be taught that the difference is very great. Suppose you have forgotten something and that others, wishing to recall it to your memory, say to you, Is it this? Is it that? offering a variety of things, as if similar. You do not, indeed, perceive that which you desire to recall, and yet do perceive that what they suggest is not it. Now when this happens to you, does it seem a genuine oblivion in every respect? For that very discernment which warns you against admitting what is false is, itself, a certain part of remembering.

A.   It seems to be so.

R.   Those in this case do not, indeed, as yet, perceive the Truth; but they cannot be misled and deceived, and they know well enough what they are seeking. Now if some one tells you that you laughed a few days after you were born, you would not venture to say it was false. And if the teller of this tale was one in whom confidence could be placed, you would give it credence, though you could not remember it; for that whole period is, for you, buried in the most profound oblivion. Or do you think otherwise?

A.   I altogether agree.

R.   This, then, differs very much from that other forgetting: but this is midway. For there is still another which is closer and more akin to the recollection of reminiscent truth. This is such as when, for example, seeing something, we recognize it as having certainly been seen before and affirm our recognition of it; but where, or how, or under what circumstances, it came to our notice, we vex ourselves to recall and rekindle. And if this happens to us in the case of a man, we go so far as to ask him when we have known him, and when he has reminded us, the whole affair suddenly floods in upon the mind like light, and no more effort is needed to cause us to remember it all. Or is this an unknown or vague experience to you?

A.   What more frequent or familiar?

35. R.   So it is with those well-learned in the liberal arts. Although they have excavated things which were, without doubt, buried in forgetfulness within themselves, *Endnote 084* and have, in a way, recovered them by learning, they are, nevertheless, not satisfied; nor do they desist from their efforts until the entire aspect of that Truth, something of whose splendor already glimmers forth in these arts, is gazed upon in its unconcealed fulness. But from them divers false colors and forms emerge and pour into the mind as upon a mirror, and often mislead those seeking and deceive them into thinking they have found all they know or seek for. Such imaginations are to be avoided with great care, and recognized as fallacies, since they vary as if in a revolving mirror of thought, while that aspect of Truth abides one and immutable. For so thought may depict to itself rectangles of one and another magnitude, and set them as if before her eyes; but that interior mind which wills to behold the true, turns itself, if it can, to that rather, according to which it judges all these to be rectangles.

A.   And what if some one says to us that the mind judges according to that which it is accustomed to see with the eyes?

R.   Whence, then, could it judge, if, indeed, it be well-trained, that any true sphere whatever is touched by a true plane surface in but one single point? Whence has any eye ever seen or ever can see such a thing, when it can be in no sort imagined by thought itself? And is not this proven when in imagination we describe the minutest possible circle, and from it lead lines to the centre? For when we have drawn two such so close that it would scarce be possible to prick between them with a needle's point and are already unable by any possible imagination to draw others in thought between them, so that they shall reach the centre without any contact; yet reason proclaims that innumerable such can be drawn, which, in these incredibly narrow spaces, can come into no contact with each other except at the centre: and so, that in the interval between each two, a circle may be inscribed! When phantasy herself cannot be persuaded of this, how much more will the eyes refuse to be! For though by the eyes the phantasm is imposed upon the thought, it is evident both that it differs greatly from the Truth, and also that while it is looked upon the Truth cannot be seen. *Endnote 085*

36. These things will be spoken of with more care and subtlety when we begin to discuss the perceptive faculty which is a department of research germane to any investigation of the life of the soul; and it shall be analyzed and argued according to our best ability. For I believe you fear in no slight degree lest human death, even though it do not kill the soul, may, nevertheless, bring in its train oblivion of all things, even — should any have been discovered — of Truth itself. *Endnote 086*

A.   How much this evil is to be feared cannot be adequately expressed! For what shall be that eternal life, — and may not death itself be preferable, — if the soul survives only so as we see it to live in the new-born boy: I say nothing of the life of the unborn, though I do not believe that to be nothing!

R.   Be of good courage! God, as we already feel, will be with us as we seek after Him: and has promised us something after this body most blessed, most abounding in Truth, without any deception!

A.   May it be as we hope!

NOTES

Endnote 001

"Furthermore, this very summer, from too great literary labor, my lungs began to be weak, and with difficulty to draw deep breaths: showing by the pains in my chest that they were affected, and refusing too loud or prolonged speaking. This had, at first, been a trial to me, for it compelled me almost of necessity to lay down that burden of teaching, or, if I could be cured and become strong again, at least to leave it off for a while. But when the full desire for leisure, that I might see that Thou art the Lord, arose, and was confirmed in me, my God, Thou knowest I even began to rejoice that I had this excuse ready, — and that not a feigned one — which might somewhat temper the offence taken by those who, for their son's good, wished me never to have the freedom of sons. Full, therefore, with such joy, I bore it till that period of time had passed — perhaps it was some twenty days — yet they were bravely borne: for the cupidity which was wont to sustain part of this weighty business had departed, and I had remained overwhelmed, had not its place been supplied by patience. Some of thy servants, my brethren, may, perchance, say that I sinned in this, in that, having once fully, and from my heart, entered on Thy warfare, I permitted myself to sit a single hour in the seat of falsehood. I will not contend. But hast not Thou, O most merciful Lord, pardoned and remitted this sin also, with my others, so horrible and deadly, in the holy water?" (Confessions, Book IX. 4.)

Endnote 002

"It has been said of Fiesole that he prayed his pictures onto the walls. It can be maintained of Augustine that his most profound thoughts regarding the first and the last things arose out of prayers; for all these matters were contained for him in God. If the same can be said of innumerable mystics down to the private communities of Madame de Guyon and Tersteegen, it is true of them because they were Augustine's disciples. But more than any one else he possessed the faculty of combining speculation about God with a contemplation of mind and soul which was not content with a few traditional categories, but analyzed the states of feeling and the contents of consciousness. Every advance in this analysis became for him at the same time an advance in the knowledge of God, and vice versa; concentration of his whole being in prayer led him to the most abstract observation, and this, in turn, changed to prayer." (Harnack, History of Dogma, p. 106.)

Endnote 003

There might be two constructions of this petition for freedom, founded, of course, on what is claimed to be Augustine's notion of it. Was it the freedom with which he had become familiar, in his long affiliation with Neoplatonism, which is the climax of mystic vision, his conception of which is seen in the famous experience with his mother at the Ostia window? I do not so conceive it. The freedom Augustine prays for is freedom from any other desire than the desire "to know God and the soul." His prayer is "Set me free from all other desires." This was his notion of freedom, as any one following the narrative of his experience up to and beyond his conversion must perceive. Harnack says: "But he only entered his proper element when he was inquiring into the practical side of spiritual life. The popular conception, beyond which even philosophers had not advanced far, was that man was a rational being who was hampered by sensuousness, but possessed a free will capable at every moment of choosing the good — a very external, dualistic view. Augustine observed the actual man. He found that the typical characteristic of the life of the soul consisted in the effort to obtain pleasure (cupido, amor); from this type no one could depart. . . . All impulses were only evolutions of this typical characteristic; sometimes they partook more of the form of passive impression, sometimes they were more of an active nature, and they were quite as true of the spiritual as of the sensuous life. According to Augustine, the will is most closely connected with this life of impulse, so that impulses can, indeed, be conceived as contents of the will, yet it is to be distinguished from them. For the will is not bound to the nexus of nature: it is a force existing above sensuous nature. It is free, in so far as it possesses formally the capacity of following or resisting the various inclinations; but concretely it is never free; that is, never free choice (liberum arbitrium), but is always conditioned by the chain of existing inclinations, which form its motives and determine it. The theoretical freedom of choice, therefore, only becomes actual freedom when desire (cupiditas, amor) of good has become the ruling motive of the will; in other words, it is only true of a good will that it is free; freedom of will and moral goodness coincide. But it follows just from this that the will truly free possesses its liberty not in caprice, but in being bound to the motive which impels to goodness ("beata necessitas boni"). This bondage is freedom, because it delivers the will from the rule of the impulses (to lower forms of good) and realizes the destiny and design of man to possess himself of true being and life. In bondage to goodness the higher appetite (appetitus), the genuine impulse of self-preservation, realizes itself, while by satisfaction "in dissipation" it brings man "bit by bit to ruin." (History of Dogma, Vol. V, pp. 112-113.)

Kant's famous dictum that there is nothing good but the good will, was first said by Augustine, who added that the good will alone is free.

A later paraphrase is Ward's: "Where rational necessity is supreme, freedom is possible and things must be intelligible. No sane man resents as a constraint normal laws of thought, normal laws of conduct, normal laws of taste, or demands that truth, goodness or beauty should be other than they are. Real freedom consists in conformity with what ought to be." (Naturalism and Agnosticism, p. 281.)

Endnote 004

Desjardins maintains concerning Augustine "that no one's teaching as to creation has shown more clearness, boldness and vigor, — avoiding the perils of dualism on the one hand and atheism on the other." We read, for example (Confessions, pp. 294, 295): "Behold, the heaven and earth are: they proclaim that they were made, for they are changed and varied. Whereas whatsoever hath not been made, and yet hath being, hath nothing in it which there was not before; this is what it is to be changed and varied. They also proclaim that they made not themselves; 'therefore we are, because we have been made; we were not, therefore, before we were, so that we could have made ourselves.' And the voice of those that speak is in itself an evidence. Thou, therefore, Lord, didst make these things. . . . But how didst Thou make them? . . . From whence couldst Thou have what Thou hadst not made, whereof to make anything? For what is, save because Thou art? Therefore Thou didst speak and they were made, and in Thy Word Thou mad'st these things."

"True reason persuaded me that I ought to remove from it all remnants of any form whatever, if I wished to conceive matter wholly without form; and I could not. For sooner could I imagine that that which should be deprived of all form was not at all, than conceive anything between form and nothing — neither formed, nor nothing, formless, nearly nothing. And my mind hence ceased to question my spirit, filled (as it was) with the images of formed bodies, and changing and varying them according to its will; and I applied myself to the bodies themselves, and looked more deeply into their mutability, by which they cease to be what they had been, and begin to be what they were not: and this same transit from form unto form, I have looked upon to be through some formless condition, not through a very nothing: but I desired to know, not to guess. And if my voice and my pen should confess the whole unto Thee, whatsoever knots Thou hast untied for me concerning this question, who of my readers would endure to take in the whole? Not yet, therefore, shall my heart cease to give Thee honor, and a song of praise, for those things which it is not able to express. For the mutability of mutable things is itself capable of all those forms into which mutable things are changed. And this mutability, what is it? Is it soul? Is it body? Is it the outer appearance of soul or body? Could it be said 'Nothing were something' and 'That which is, is not,' I would say that this were it; and yet in some manner was it already, since it could receive these visible and compound shapes. And whence and in what manner was this, unless from Thee, from whom are all things, in so far as they are? . . . Thou wast, and there was naught else from which Thou didst create heaven and earth." (Confessions, pp. 322, 323.)

If some substitutions for "Creator," "forms," "almost nothing," "transit," "God," "mutability," should be made by such terms as twentieth-century science uses, such as "evolution," "conservation of energy," "mind stuff," "force," "ether" and "reality," the above could be fairly well translated into its formulæ.

Fairbairn says: "And when he [J. S. Mill] proceeded to define matter as 'the permanent possibility of sensation' . . . how, without the sentient consciousness, could we have matter? And when later he resolved mind into 'a permanent possibility of feeling,' he carefully forgot that he had assumed mind, its expectancy and associative laws, in order that he might explain matter as 'the permanent possibility of sensation.' . . . He would have been more consistent had he, with Berkeley, confessed spirit to be the one solid and enduring entity, and matter a mere idea. This was what he meant, but what he could not say without being forced to the theistic conclusion of his great predecessor. . . . But science was suddenly seized with a speculative passion, begotten of two great doctrines — the conservation of energy, and evolution; . . . thinkers like Mr. Lewes forgot their paralyzed nescience and began to lay the 'foundations of a creed.' Men of science became adventurous world-builders; awed us by natural histories of creation, over-awed us by visions of our long descent, and the easy elegance with which they could leap the boundary which divided the organic from the inorganic kingdom, and find in matter 'the promise and the potency of every form and quality of life.' Goethe's words were gratefully recalled: 'Matter can never exist and be operative without spirit, nor spirit without matter.' So were Schleicher's: 'There is neither matter nor spirit in the customary sense, but only one thing which is at the same time both.'. Then we had the despairing but descriptive phrase of the late Professor Clifford, 'mind stuff,' and Professor Bain's 'One substance with two sets of properties; two sides, the physical and the mental; a double-faced unity.'

"But what is this save carrying back into the beginning the dualism of the living consciousness? It did not define or describe the primordial stuff which constituted and created the world, but only expressed a distinction which came into being with the conscious self. . . . It is significant that modern physics, perhaps the most audacious in speculation of all the sciences, nor chemistry, possibly the most skilled in the secrets of Nature, has advanced us here a single step beyond Democritus; . . . to matter, as science must conceive it, causation of life, not to speak of mind, is a sheer impossibility. . . . As Tyndall once said: 'A man can as little prove any causal relation between the two as he can lift himself by his own waistband. . . . We cannot conceive either nature or its creative work otherwise than through mind. . . . To affirm the transcendence of thought is to affirm the priority of spirit, for spirit is but thought made concrete — translated, as it were, into a personal and creative energy. . . . And how can we better express this thought in its highest concrete form than by the ancient name, God?' " (The Philosophy of Christian Religion, p. 51, et seq.) And Ward: "How far below us, how far above, the historical extends, we cannot tell. But above it there can be only God as the living unity of all, and below it no longer things, but only the connecting, conserving acts of the One Supreme." (Naturalism and Agnosticism, II, p. 280.)

On the whole, the latest of latter day speculators seem to have less difficulty than Augustine, in conceiving of a creation of matter. Sir Oliver Lodge says: "It is quite easy to conceive them [the atoms] broken up, the identity of the electron lost, its substance resolved into the original ether, without parts or individual properties. If this happened within our ken, we should have to confess that the properties of matter were gone, and that hence anything that could by any stretch of language be called 'matter' was destroyed, since no identifying property remained. The discovery of such an event may lie in the science of the future . . . in other words, the destruction and the creation of matter are well within the range of scientific conception, and may be within the realm of experimental possiility." (Life and Matter, p. 28.)

An excellent discussion of Augustine's theory of creation, as related to that of the Neoplatonic doctrine, may be found in Chapter IV of Saint Augustin et La Neoplatonisme, by L. Grandgeorge, Paris, 1896.

Endnote 005

"Augustine never tires of realizing the beauty (pulchrum) and fitness (aptum) of creation, of regarding the universe as an ordered work of art, in which the gradations are as admirable as the contrasts. The individual and evil are lost to view in the notion of beauty; nay, God himself is the eternal, the old and new, the only beauty." (History of Dogma, V, p. 114.)

Endnote 006

"As yet I knew not that evil was naught but a privation of good, until in the end it ceases altogether to be." (Confessions, p. 46.)

"No nature at all is evil, and this is a name for nothing but the want of good." (City of God, I, p. 462.)

Endnote 007

"If we ask why He made it, 'it was good.' Neither is there any author more excellent than God, nor any skill more efficacious than the word of God, nor any cause better than that good might be created by the good God. This also Plato has assigned as the most sufficient reason for the creation of the world, that good works might be made by a good God. . . .

"This cause, however, of a good creation, namely, the goodness of God, . . . has not been recognized by some heretics, because there are, forsooth, many things, such as fire, frost, wild beasts, etc., which do not suit but injure this thin-blooded and frail mortality of our flesh, which is at present under just punishment. They do not consider how admirable these things are in their own places, how excellent in their own natures, how beautifully adjusted to the rest of creation, and how much grace they contribute to the universe by their own contributions as to a commonwealth; and how serviceable they are even to ourselves, if we use them with a knowledge of their fit adaptations. . . . And thus Divine Providence admonishes us not foolishly to vituperate things, but to investigate their utility with care; and, where our mental capacity or infirmity is at fault, to believe that there is a utility, though hidden, as we have experienced that there were other things which we all but failed to discover." (City of God, I, pp. 461, 462.)

Endnote 008

"And to Thee is there nothing at all evil, and not only to Thee, but to Thy whole creation; because there is nothing without which can break in and mar that order which Thou hast appointed it. But in the parts thereof, some things, because they harmonize not with others, are considered evil: whereas those very things harmonize with others, and are good, and in themselves are good. And all these things which do not harmonize together harmonize with the inferior part which we call earth, having its own cloudy and windy sky concordant to it. Far be it from me, then, to say 'These things should not be.' For should I see nothing but these, I should indeed desire better; but yet, if only for these, ought I to praise Thee; . . . I did not now desire better things, because I was thinking of all; and with a better judgment I reflected that the things above were better than those below, but that all were better than those above alone. There is no wholeness in them whom aught of thy creation displeaseth; no more than there was in me, when many things which Thou madest displeased me." (Confessions, pp. 160, 161.)

Endnote 009

Augustine says in criticism of this passage: "One can reply that there are men who are not pure and yet know many things, for I have not taken pains here to define the True, which pure souls alone know, and also what I mean by knowing." (Retractations, Book I, chap. 4.)

Endnote 010

"Not this common light, which all flesh may look upon, nor, as it were, a greater one of the same kind, as though the brightness of this should be much more resplendent, and with its greatness fill up all things. Not like this was that Light, but different, yea, very different from all these. . . . He who knows the Truth knows that Light; and he that knows it knoweth Eternity. Love knoweth it. O Eternal Truth, and true Love and loved Eternity!" (Confessions, pp. 157, 158.)

Endnote 011

"And I viewed the other things below Thee, and perceived that they neither altogether are, nor altogether are not. They are, indeed, because they are from Thee; but are not, because they are not what Thou art. For that truly is which remains immutably. It is good, then, for me to cleave unto God, for if I remain not in Him, neither shall I in myself; but He, remaining in Himself, reneweth all things." (Confessions, p. 159.)

Constantly Augustine affirms that God alone is true Being, or to use the modern word of theologians, philosophers and scientists alike, Reality. It is indeed difficult to distinguish this doctrine of God, never enunciated, however, in the form of systematic dogma, but rather as a saturation of his thought and feeling, — personal sine qua non — from actual Monism. In its last analysis it logically abstracts every creature from the realm of reality, to leave God All in All.

Endnote 012

"Now it was expedient that man should be at first so created, as to have it in his power both to will what was right and to will what was wrong; not without reward if he willed the former, and not without punishment if he willed the latter." (Enchiridion, p. 249.)

"For the will is in them [impulses of the passional nature] all; yea, none of them is anything else than will. For what are desire and joy but a volition of consent to the things we wish? And what are fear and sadness but a volition of aversion from the things which we do not wish? But when consent takes the form of seeking to possess the things we wish this is called desire; and when consent takes the form of enjoying the things we wish this is called joy. In like manner, when we turn with aversion from that which we do not wish to happen, this volition is termed fear; and when we turn away from that which has happened against our will, this act of will is called sorrow." (City of God, II, p. 9.)

It is interesting to notice the agreement of present-day psychology of the will, with this of Augustine: Mr. James carries it into the sphere of opinion, and enunciates a definite (?) dogma of Will to Believe, which might be a paraphrase of Augustine's volition of consent to the things we wish.

Endnote 013

"So God created man in His own image, in the image of God created He him." (Genesis, 1: 27.)

"But we must find in the soul of man, i. e. the rational or intellectual soul, that image of the Creator which is immortally implanted in its immortality. For as the immortality itself of the soul is spoken with a qualification; since the soul too has its proper death, when it lacks a blessed life, which is to be called the true life of the soul; but it is therefore called immortal, because it never ceases to live with some life or other, even when it is most miserable; — so, although reason or intellect is at one time torpid in it, at another appears small, and at another great, yet the human soul is never anything save rational or intellectual; and hence, if it is made after the image of God in respect to this, that it is able to use reason and intellect in order to understand and behold God, then from the moment when that nature so marvellous and so great began to be, whether this image be so worn out as to be almost none at all, or whether it be obscure and defaced, or bright and beautiful, certainly it always is." (Trinity, p. 350.)

Endnote 014

Villemain quotes Augustine's words: "God is not only the Creator, but the Country of the soul," and adds: "Without doubt this inspired the sublime expression of Malebranche, 'God is the place of spirits, as space is the place of bodies.' "

Endnote 015

"But where, during all those years, and out of what deep and secret retreat was my free will summoned forth in a moment, whereby I gave my neck to Thy 'easy yoke' and my shoulders to Thy 'light burden,' O Christ Jesus, my strength and my Redeemer?" (Confessions, pp. 206, 207.)

Endnote 016

"But behold, Thou wert close behind thy fugitives, at once God of vengeance and Fountain of mercies, who turnest us to Thyself by wondrous means." (Confessions, p. 62.)

"Oh, let truth, the light of my heart, not my own darkness, speak unto me! I have descended to that, and am darkened. But thence, even thence, did I love Thee. I went astray, and remembered Thee. I heard Thy voice behind me, bidding me return, and scarcely did I hear it for the tumults of the unquiet ones. And now, behold, I return burning and panting after Thy fountain. Let no one prohibit me! of this will I drink, and so have life. Let me not be my own life! from myself have I badly lived — death was I unto myself: in Thee do I revive." (Confessions, p. 325.)

Endnote 017

"A fervent prayer precedes this meditation and disposes the soul to a tranquil enthusiasm of which it has need in order to thoroughly see and recognize itself. There is here, in fact, a sort of ecstasy of reflection which in nothing resembles the violent emotion experienced in the garden at Milan at the crisis of repentance and faith. His resolution is taken; effort is no longer necessary, and the invocation, although ardent, breathes of calm. It is the movement of a soul committed to no backward step. Reason, herself, has told Augustine to pray to the God of truth, the God of wisdom, the Father of beatitude, of the good, of the beautiful, of intelligible Light. He prays with confidence, with serenity. . . and under the auspices of this pious initiation, he seeks in fact knowledge, in taking up this dialogue with Reason." (Villemain, Tableau de l'Éloquence Chrétienne au IVe Siècle, p. 402.)

Endnote 018

"In these words Augustine has briefly formulated the aim of his spiritual life. That was the truth for which 'the marrow of his soul sighed.' All truth was contained for him in the perception of God. After a brief period of sore doubting, he was firm as a rock in the conviction that there was a God, and that he was the supreme good (summum bonum); but who he was, and how he was to be found were to him the great questions. He was first snatched from the night of uncertainty by Neoplatonism; the Manichean notion of God had proved itself to be false, since its God was not absolute and omnipotent. . . . He was saved from scepticism by perceiving that even if the whole of eternal experience was subject to doubt, the facts of the inner life remained and demanded an explanation leading to certainty. There is no evil, but we are afraid, and this fear is certainly an evil. There is no visible object of faith, but we see faith in us. Thus — in his theory of perception — God and the soul entered into the closest union, and this union confirmed him in his belief in their metaphysical connection. Henceforth the investigation of the life of the soul was to him a theological necessity. No examination seemed to him to be indifferent: he sought to obtain divine knowledge from every quarter." (History of Dogma, V, p. 110, et seq.)

Endnote 019

Augustine writes to his dear friend Nebridius: "Although you know my mind well, you are perhaps not aware how much I long to enjoy your society. This great blessing, however, God will some day bestow on me. I have read your letter, so genuine in its utterances, in which you complain of your being in solitude, and, as it were, forsaken by your friends, in whose society you found the sweetest charm of life. But what else can I suggest to you than that which I am persuaded is already your exercise? Commune with your own soul, and raise it up, as far as you are able, unto God. For in Him you hold us also by a firmer bond, not by means of bodily images which we must meanwhile be content to use in remembering each other, but by means of that faculty of thought through which we realize the fact of our separation from each other." (Letters, I, p. 20.)

Augustine's love of friends and friendship is always conspicuous; his lament for the friend of his youth recalls Milton's grief for his friend lost at sea (see Lycidas), but a comparison is impossible. "At this sorrow my heart was utterly darkened, and whatever I looked upon was death. My native country was a torture to me, and my father's house a wondrous unhappiness; and whatsoever I had participated in with him, wanting him, turned into a frightful torture. Mine eyes sought him everywhere, but he was not granted them; and I hated all places because he was not in them; nor could they now say to me 'Behold he is coming,' as they did when he was alive and absent. . . . I was astonished that other mortals lived, since he whom I loved, as if he would never die, was dead; and I wondered still more that I, who was to him a second self, could live when he was dead. Well did one say of his friend 'Thou half of my soul,' for I felt that my soul and his soul were but one soul in two bodies; and consequently my life was a horror to me, because I would not live in half. And therefore, perchance, was I afraid to die, lest he should die wholly whom I had so greatly loved." (Confessions, pp. 62-65.)

Augustine tells us what "is loved in friends:" "to discourse and jest with them; to indulge in an interchange of kindnesses; to read together pleasant books; together to trifle, and together to be earnest; to differ, at times, without ill-humour, as a man would do with his own self; and even by the infrequency of these differences to give zest to our more frequent consentings; sometimes teaching, sometimes being taught; longing for the absent with impatience, and welcoming the coming with joy. These and similar expressions, emanating from the hearts of those who loved and were beloved in return, by the countenance, the tongue, the eyes, and a thousand pleasing movements, were so much fuel to melt our souls together, and out of many to make but one." (Confessions, p. 67.)

Endnote 020

"Alypius was born in the same town as myself, his parents being of the highest rank there, but he being younger than I. For he had studied under me, first when I taught in our town, and afterwards at Carthage, and esteemed me highly, because I appeared to him good and learned; and I esteemed him for his innate love of virtue, which, in one of no great age, was sufficiently eminent. (Confessions, p. 121.)

Alypius was converted and baptized when Augustine was and continued his companion for some time after; was Bishop of Thagaste, their common birthplace, when Augustine was Bishop of Hippo. Augustine calls him the "brother of his heart" and undertook to write his life. Bishop to bishop, he addresses him: "My Lord Alypius most blessed, my brother and colleague, beloved and longed for with sincere veneration." (Letters, I, p. 346.)

Endnote 021

"Philosophers have been far too apt to jump to the conclusion that because energy is constant, therefore no guidance is possible, so that all psychological or other interference is precluded. Physicists, however, know better. . . . It has gradually dawned upon me that the reason why philosophers who are well acquainted with physical or dynamical science are apt to fall into the error of supposing that mental and vital interference with the material world is impossible . . . is because all such interference is naturally and necessarily excluded from scientific methods and treatises . . . . determinateness is not part of the essence of dynamical doctrine; it is arrived at by the tacit assumption that no undynamical or hyper-dynamical agencies exist; in short, by that process of abstraction which is invariably necessary for simplicity, and indeed for possibility, of methodical human treatment." (Lodge, Life and Matter, pp. 20, 140.)

"In a word, concisely to express the scope of that regularity which science postulates, we must say, as Kant has done, not only In mundo non datur casus, but also, In mundo non datur fatum. Nothing happens by blind chance, and also nothing happens by blind necessity." (Ward, Naturalism and Agnosticism, Vol. II, p. 252.)

Endnote 022

At the time this was written, Augustine was yet a catechumen. He does not speak, for he does not think, as a Catholic theologian. The moral crisis was past in his conversion; he was "cleaving unto God." But the mental crisis had no violent end; his intellectual habits and holdings of that period changed slowly, were indeed, never wholly lost. He had acquired the "good will" once for all, but had only entered upon the philosophic revolution, which was the Christian evolution, the one an agony of death, the other an agony of birth. Platonic ideas haunted him, even while he sifted them. Later he wrote the story of his acquaintance with Plato and his school in clear terms, but not wholly those of an ecclesiastic (Confessions, p. 152 et seq.). Later still, as Bishop and Defender of the Faith, he writes again of Plato. (City of God, I, p. 306 et seq.)

He proclaims his reverence for his first great master: "It is evident that none come nearer to us than the Platonists." "The theology of St. Augustine, like his philosophy, is only the expression of the life and struggles of his soul. He has been a Platonist, because it is in Plato that he has found the light; he has become Christian, because it is in Christ that he has found strength. The first has revealed to him the invisible world; the second has torn him away from the world of the senses. Without Plato, he would have remained immersed in Manichean materialism; without Christ he would not have been rescued from the bondage of the flesh." (Paul Janet, Introduction to Confessions.)

Plotinus, too, was much revered by Augustine. (See Saint Augustin et La Neoplatonisme, by L. Grandgeorge, Paris, 1896.) Nebridius writes to Augustine (Letters, I, p. 11): "Your letters I have great pleasure in keeping as carefully as my own eyes. For they are great, not indeed in length, but in the greatness of the subjects discussed in them, and in the great ability with which the truth in regard to these subjects is demonstrated. They shall bring to my ear the voice of Christ, and the teaching of Plato and of Plotinus."

Endnote 023

"The Soliloquies offer numerous allusions to Academic scepticism which St. Augustine had hitherto professed. Having been for long seduced by this doctrine, he considered it as the first enemy which his new born faith ought to overcome. Cicero, the most important representative of this school, exposes concisely its doctrines in Book II of his Treatise Concerning Duty, Chapter 2. 'It is pretended that there are things certain, and things uncertain: we are of another opinion, and say that there are things probable and things improbable.' " (Soliloquies, Pelissier's translation, Note 13.)

Endnote 024

Augustine says of his first great work, Contra Academicos, written at Casciacum: "Whatever be the value of those treatises what I most rejoice in is, not that I have vanquished the Academicians, as you express it (using the language rather of friendly partiality than of truth), but that I have broken and cast away from me the odious bonds by which I was kept back from the nourishing breasts of philosophy, through despair of attaining that truth which is the food of the soul." (Letters, I, p. 3.)

Endnote 025

Apropos of "happiness," I allow myself to insert this delightful portrait:

"You have almost made me believe, not indeed, that I am happy, — for that is the heritage of the wise alone, — but that I am at least in a sense happy: as we apply the designation man to beings who deserve the name only in a sense if compared with Plato's ideal man, or speak of things which we see as round or square, although they differ widely from the perfect figure which is discerned by the mind of a few. I read your letter beside my lamp after supper; immediately after which I lay down, but not at once to sleep; for on my bed I meditated long and talked thus with myself — Augustine addressing and answering Augustine:

" 'Is it not true as Nebridius affirms, that I am happy?'

" 'Absolutely true it cannot be, for that I am still far from wise, he himself would not deny.'

" 'But may not a happy life be the lot even of those who are not wise?'

" 'That is scarcely possible; because, in that case, lack of wisdom would be a small misfortune, and not, as it actually is, the one and only source of unhappiness.'

" 'How, then, did Nebridius come to esteem me happy? Was it that, after reading these little books of mine, he ventured to pronounce me wise?'

" 'Surely the vehemence of joy could not make him so rash, especially seeing that he is a man to whose judgment I well know so much weight is to be attached. I have it now; he wrote what he thought would be most gratifying to me, because he had been gratified by what I had written in those treatises; and he wrote in a joyful mood, without accurately weighing the sentiments entrusted to his joyous pen.'

" 'What, then, would he have said if he had read my Soliloquies?'

" 'He would have rejoiced with much more exultatation, and yet could find no loftier name to bestow on me than this which he has already given in calling me happy. All at once, then, he has lavished on me the highest possible name, and has not reserved a single word to add to my praises, if at any time he were made by me more joyful than he is now. See what joy does.' . . .

" 'Surely there is in this something which might reward further investigation; but meanwhile, I must sleep. Moreover, if I seem to Nebridius to be happy, it is not because I seek, but because perchance I have found something. What then is that something? Is it that chain of reasoning which I am wont so to caress as if it were my sole treasure, and in which perhaps I take too much delight? . . . Perhaps it is on account of reasonings such as these that I have been judged by my own Nebridius to be, if not absolutely happy, at least in a sense happy. Let me also judge myself to be happy; for what do I lose thereby, or why should I grudge to think well of my own estate?' Thus I talked with myself, then prayed according to my custom and fell asleep." (Letters.)

Endnote 026

"Thus Augustine, in abandoning his soul to all the fervor of religious faith, retained his enthusiasm for knowledge: he is uplifted to God by philosophic contemplation, as by piety; by reasoning, as by love. . . . Raised to virtue, not by faith alone, but by reasoning as well, behold here the labor of a well-instructed soul! The intellect disciplined by study focuses to the knowledge of God all human sciences as so many routes, which from different points of the horizon lead toward the same temple. The soul dominated by virtue, which gives itself to calm and harmony, will have a recompense, of which Augustine cannot speak without a ravishing enthusiasm. 'It will dare to see God,' he exclaims, 'and the source whence emanates the true, the Father Himself of Truth. Great God! what gazes will be raised toward Thee! How pure, how noble will they be! what of strength, of constancy, of serenity, of beatitude, will they have! How can we think of, how speak of them? We have for them only every-day words, profaned by miserable use.' " (Tableau de l'Éloquence Chrétienne au IVe Siècle, pp. 399, 400.)

Endnote 027

"I asked the earth; and it answered 'I am not He,' and whatsoever are therein made the same confession. I asked the sea and the deeps, and the creeping things that lived, and they replied 'We are not thy God, seek higher than we.' I asked the breezy air, and the universal air with its inhabitants answered 'Anaximenes was deceived, I am not God.' I asked the heavens, the sun, moon and stars: 'Neither,' say they, 'are we the God whom thou seekest.' And I answered unto all these things which stand about the door of my flesh 'Ye have told me concerning my God. That ye are not He; tell me something about Him,' and with a loud voice they exclaimed 'He made us.' My questioning was my observing of them; and their beauty was their reply. And I directed my thoughts to myself and said 'Who art thou?' And I answered 'A man.' And lo! in me there appear both body and soul, the one without, the other within. By which of these should I seek my God, whom I had sought through the body from earth to heaven, as far as I was able to send messengers — the beams of mine eyes? But the better part is that which is inner: for to it, as both president and judge, did all these my corporeal messengers render the answers of heaven and earth and all things therein, who said 'We are not God, but he made us.' These things was my inner man cognizant of by the ministry of the outer: I, the inner man, knew all this — I, the soul, through the senses of my body. . . . By my soul itself will I mount up unto Him." (Confessions, pp. 243-244.)

"Thence, again, I passed on to the reasoning faculty, unto which whatever is received from the senses of the body, is referred to be judged, which also, finding itself to be variable in me, raised itself up to its own intelligence, and from habit drew away my thoughts, withdrawing itself from the crowds of contradictory phantasms; that so it might find out that light by which it was besprinkled." (Confessions, pp. 163, 164.)

Endnote 028

"That light which illumines the soul, he tells us in his De Gen. ad Lit. (Book XII, p. 31) is God Himself, from whom all light cometh; and though created in His image and likeness, when it tries to discover Him, palpitat infirmitate et minus valet. . . . In his De Civ. Dei (X, 2), he quotes from Plotinus in regard to the Platonic doctrine as to enlightenment from on high. He says: "Plotinus, commenting on Plato, repeatedly and strongly asserts that not even the soul, which they believe to be the soul of the world, derives its blessedness from any other source than we do, viz.: from that Light which is distinct from it and created it, and by whose intelligible illumination it enjoys light in things intelligible. He also compares those spiritual things to the vast and conspicuous heavenly bodies, as if God were the sun, and the soul the moon; for they suppose that the moon derives its light from the sun. That great Platonist, therefore, says that the rational soul, or rather the intellectual soul, — in which class he comprehends the souls of the blessed immortals who inhabit heaven, — has no nature superior to it save God, the Creator of the world and the soul itself, and that these heavenly spirits derive their blessed life, and the light of truth, from the same source as ourselves, agreeing with the gospel where we read 'There was a man sent from God, whose name was John. The same came for a witness, to bear witness of that Light, that through Him all might believe. He was not that Light, but that he might bear witness of the Light. That was the true Light which lighteth every man that cometh into the world' (John 1: 6-9), — a distinction which sufficiently proves that the rational or intellectual soul, such as John had, cannot be its own light, but needs to receive illumination from another, the true Light." (Confessions, p. 164, note.)

Endnote 029

At this time Augustine was not more a a Catholic theologian than a Catholic theosophist. The methods suggested by this statement that "the vision of God can be attained even while still in the body," betray his long affiliation with Neoplatonism. In this connection Harnack refers to "suggestions" in this direction found in the Confessions (VII, 13-16, 23), and says: (History of Dogma, V, p. 111, note) "Here is described the intellectual 'exercise' of the observation of the *mutabilia* leading to the *incommutabile*. 'And thus, with the flash of a trembling glance, it arrived at that which is. And then I saw Thy invisible things understood by the things that are made (this now becomes his dominant saying). But I was not able to fix my gaze thereon; and my infirmity being beaten back, I was thrown again on my accustomed habits, carrying along with me naught but a loving memory thereof, and an appetite (quite as in Plotinus) for what I had, as it were, smelt the odour of, but was not yet able to eat.' But, again, in his famous dialogue with his mother in Ostia, a regular Neoplatonic 'exercise' is really described which ends with ecstasy (*attigimus veri tatem modice toto ictu cordis*)." (If not familiar to the reader, he will be grateful for the insertion here of a part of this dialogue, which has been made, if possible, even more vivid in its portrayal of Monica and her son at the window in Ostia overlooking the sea, by the famous canvas of Ary Scheffer.)

"If to any man the tumult of the flesh were silenced — silenced the phantasies of earth, waters, and air; silenced, too, the poles; yea, the very soul be silenced to herself, and go beyond herself by not thinking of herself, — silenced fancies and imaginary revelations, every tongue, and every sign, and whatsoever exists by passing away, since, if any could hearken, all these say, 'We created not ourselves but were created by Him who abideth forever:' If, having uttered this, they now should be silenced, having only quickened our ears to Him who created them, and He alone speak, not by them, but by Himself, that we may hear His word, not by fleshly tongue, nor angelic voice, nor sound of thunder, nor the obscurity of a similitude, but might hear Him — Him whom in these we love — without these, like as we two [his mother and himself at the Ostia window] now strained ourselves, and with rapid thought touched on that Eternal Wisdom which remaineth over all. If this could be sustained, and other visions of a far different kind be withdrawn, and this one ravish and absorb, and envelope its be holder, amid these inward joys, so that his life might be eternally like that one moment of knowledge which we now sighed after, were not this 'Enter thou into the joy of thy Lord? but when shall this be?' " (Confessions, Book IX, chap. 10.)

Harnack adds (History of Dogma, V, p. 111, note): "We afterwards meet extremely seldom with anything of the same kind in Augustine: on the other hand, the anti-Manichean writing still show many echoes ('se rapere in deum,' 'rapi in deum,' 'volitare,' 'amplexus dei'). Reuter says rightly (p. 472) that these are unusual expressions, only occurring exceptionally. But he must have forgotten the passages in the Confessions, when he adds that no instructions are given as to the method to be followed."

The Soliloquies were written in 386, the Confessions in 400, the four books on Christian Doctrine in 426. It is interesting to compare the instructions in each for the attainment of wisdom or the vision of God, and to note how the Neoplatonist survives in all, inextricably confused with the Church-father. (See Soliloquies above: Confessions, Book VII, 13-16, 23; Book IX, 23, 25; and Christian Doctrine, p. 39.) The Church-father emerges more clearly, and the theosophist retires, in his criticism of Porphyry (City of God, p. 430 et seq.).

Endnote 030

"But sight shall displace faith: and hope shall be swallowed up in that perfect bliss to which we shall come: love, on the other hand, shall wax greater when these others fail. For if we love by faith that which as yet we see not, how much more shall we love it when we begin to see! And if we love by hope that which as yet we have not reached, how much more shall we love it when we reach it! For there is this great difference between things temporal and things eternal, that a temporal object is valued more before we possess it, and begins to prove worthless the moment we attain it, because it does not satisfy the soul, which has its only true and sure resting-place in eternity: an eternal object, on the other hand, is loved with greater ardour when it is in possession than while it is still an object of desire, for no one in his longing for it can set a higher value on it than really belongs to it, so as to think it comparatively worthless when he finds it of less value than he thought; on the contrary, however high the value any man may set upon it when he is on his way to possess it, he will find it, when it comes into his possession, of higher value still." (Christian Doctrine, p. 32.)

Endnote 031

Augustine tells us such a community had been planned: "And many of us friends, consulting on and abhorring the turbulent vexations of human life, had considered and now almost determined upon living at ease and separate from the turmoil of men. And this was to be obtained in this way; we were to bring whatever we could severally procure, and make a common household, so that, through the sincerity of our friendship, nothing should belong more to one than the other; but the whole, being derived from all, should as a whole belong to each, and the whole unto all. It seemed to us that this society might consist of ten persons, some of whom were very rich, especially Romanianus, our townsman, an intimate friend of mine from his childhood, whom grave business matters had then brought up to Court; who was the most earnest of us all for this project, and whose voice was of great weight in commending it, because his estate was far more ample than that of the rest. We had arranged, too, that two officers should be chosen yearly, for the providing of all necessary things, whilst the rest were left undisturbed. But when we began to reflect whether the wives which some of us had already, and others hoped to have, would permit this, all that plan, which was being so well framed, broke to pieces in our hands, and was utterly wrecked and cast aside. Thence we fell again to sighs and groans, and our steps to follow the broad and beaten ways of the world." (Confessions, p. 135.)

Endnote 032

"In the ordinary course of study, I lighted upon a certain book of Cicero, whose language, though not his heart, almost all admire. This book of his contains an exhortation to philosophy, and is called Hortensius. This book, in truth, changed my affections, and turned my prayers to Thyself, O Lord, and made me have other hopes and desires. Worthless suddenly became every vain hope to me; and, with an incredible warmth of heart,

I yearned for an immortality of wisdom, and began now to arise that I might return to Thee." (Confessions, p. 41.)

Endnote 033

"I was entangled in the life of this world, clinging to dull hopes of a beauteous wife, the pomp of riches, the emptiness of honors, and the other hurtful and destructive pleasures." (De Util. Credendi, Sec. 3.) "After I had shaken off the Manicheans and escaped, especially when I had crossed the sea, the Academics long detained me tossing in the waves, winds from all quarters beating against my helm. And so I came to this shore, and there found a pole-star to whom to entrust myself. For I often observed in the discourses of our priest (Ambrose), and sometimes in yours (Theodorus), that you had no corporeal notions when you thought of God, or even of the soul, which of all things is next to God. But I was withheld, I own, from casting myself speedily into the bosom of true wisdom by the alluring hopes of marriage and honors; meaning, when I had obtained these, to press (as few singularly happy had before me), with oar and sail into that haven, and there rest." (De Vita Beata, Sec. 4.)

Endnote 034

"Since that vehement flame which was about to seize me as yet was not, I thought that by which I was slowly kindled was the very greatest. When lo! certain books, when they had distilled a very few drops of most precious unguent on that tiny flame, it is past belief, Romanianus, past belief, and perhaps past what even you believe of me (and what could I say more?) nay, to myself also is it past belief, what a conflagration of myself they lighted. What ambition, what human show, what empty love of fame, or lastly, what incitement or band of this mortal life could hold me then? I turned speedily and wholly back into myself. I cast but a glance, I confess, as one passing on, upon that religion which was implanted into us as boys, and interwoven with our very inmost selves; but she drew me unknowing to herself. So, then, stumbling, hurrying, hesitating, I seized the Apostle Paul: 'for never,' said I, 'could they have wrought such things, or lived as it is plain they did live, if their writings and arguments were opposed to this so high good.' I read the whole most intently and carefully. But then, never so little light having been shed thereon, such a countenance of wisdom gleamed upon me, that if I could exhibit it — I say not to you, who ever hungeredst after her, though unknown — but to your very adversary . . . casting aside and abandoning whatever now stimulates him so keenly to whatsoever pleasures, he would, amazed, panting, enkindled, fly to her Beauty." (Con. Acad. II, 5.)

Endnote 035

"This much hast Thou taught me, that I should bring myself to take food as medicine. . . . And whereas health is the reason of eating and drinking, there joineth itself as an handmaid a perilous delight, which mostly tries to precede it, in order that I may do for her sake what I say I do, or desire to do, for health's sake. Nor have both the same limit; for what is sufficient for health is too little for pleasure. And oftentimes it is doubtful whether it be the necessary care of the body which still asks nourishment, or whether a sensual snare of desire offers its ministry. In this uncertainty does my unhappy soul rejoice, and therein prepares an excuse as a defence, glad that it doth not appear what may be sufficient for the moderation of health, that so under the pretence of health it may conceal the business of pleasure. These temptations do I daily endeavour to resist, and I summon Thy right hand to my help, and refer my excitements to Thee, because as yet I have no resolve in this matter." (Confessions, p. 268.)

Endnote 036

"And what more could we desire? We have crowds of influential friends, though we have nothing else, and if we make haste a presidentship may be offered us; and a wife with some money that she increase not our expenses; and this shall be the height of desire. Many men, who are great and worthy of imitation, have applied themselves to the study of wisdom in the marriage state." (Confessions, p. 131.)

Endnote 037

"But what they assert is this: they say that all fools are mad, as all dunghills stink; not that they always do so, but stir them, and you will perceive it." (Cicero — Tusculum Disputations, Book IV, 24, translated by C. D. Yonge.)

Endnote 038

"Nor was that wound of mine as yet cured which had been caused by the separation from my former mistress, but after inflammation and most acute anguish it mortified, and the pain became numbed, but more desperate." (Confessions, p. 136.)

Endnote 039

"For those who are most truly wise, and whom alone it is right to pronounce happy, have maintained that fortune's favours ought not to be the objects of either fear or desire." (Letters, p. 8.)

Endnote 040

"Is it true, my beloved Augustine, that you are spending your strength and patience on the affairs of your fellow citizens (in Thagaste), and that the leisure from distractions which you so earnestly desired is still withheld from you? Who, I would like to know, are the men who thus take advantage of your good nature, and trespass on your time? I believe that they do not know what you love most and long for. Have you no friend at hand to tell them what your heart is set upon? Will neither Romanianus nor Lucinianus do this? Let them hear me at all events. I will proclaim aloud: I will protest that God is the supreme object of your love, and that your heart's desire is to be His servant, and to cleave to Him. Fain would I persuade you to come to my home in the country, and rest here: I shall not be afraid of being denounced as a robber by those countrymen of yours, whom you love only too well, and by whom you are too warmly loved in return." (Letters, I, p. 11. Nebridius to Augustine.)

Endnote 041

. . . "It is a question whether man is to be loved by man for his own sake, or for the sake of something else. If it is for his own sake, we enjoy him; if it is for the sake of something else, we use him. It seems to me, then, that he is to be loved for the sake of something else. For if a thing is to be loved for its own sake, then in the enjoyment of it consists a happy life, the hope of which at least, if not yet the reality, is our comfort in the present time. But a curse is pronounced on him who places his hope in man." (Christian Doctrine, I, p. 18.)

Endnote 042

"Why are there times in which, speaking, we do not fear death, and silent, even desire it? I say to you — for I would not say it to every one — to you whose visits to the upper world I know well, 'Will you, who have often felt how sweetly the soul lives when it dies to all mere bodily affections, deny that it is possible for the whole life of man to become at length so exempt from fear, that he may be justly called wise?'" (Letters, p. 24.)

Endnote 043

"Thou didst at that time torture me with toothache; and when it had become so exceeding great that I was not able to speak, it came into my heart to urge all my friends who were present to pray for me to Thee, the God of all manner of health. And I wrote it down on wax, and gave it to them to read. Presently, as with submissive desire we bowed our knees, that pain departed. But what pain? Or how did it depart? I confess to being much afraid, my Lord my God, seeing that from my earliest years I had not experienced such pain." (Confessions, IX, p. 216.)

Endnote 044

"I was wrong in saying that more than one way led to wisdom; there is none outside of Jesus who says: 'I am the way.'" (Retractations, I, chap. 4.)

Endnote 045

"And I entered, and with the eye of my soul (such as it was) saw above the same eye of my soul, above my mind, the Unchangeable Light. Not this common light . . . not like this was that light, but different, yea, very different from all these." (Confessions, p. 157.) (See note 28 above.)

Endnote 046

"Such a son ascends to wisdom, which is the seventh and last step, and which he enjoys in peace and tranquillity. For the fear of God is the beginning of wisdom. From that beginning, then, till we reach wisdom itself, our way is by the steps now described." (Christian Doctrine, p. 40.)

This "order" (see note 29) was variously conceived at different stages in Augustine's evolution, as we have already seen.

Endnote 047

Augustine voices this, his one positive assertion, nowhere better than in what Harnack calls the "glorious sentence" in the prayer with which he enters upon these soliloquies: "I know nothing other than that the fleeting and the fading should be spurned, the fixed and eternal sought after." His correspondence with Nebridius repeats constantly the same conviction.

"With what has the understanding to contend?"

"With the senses."

"Must we then resist the senses with all our might?"

"Certainly."

"What, then, if the things with which the senses acquaint us give us pleasure?"

"We must prevent them from doing so."

"How?"

"By acquiring the habit of doing without them and desiring better things." (Letters, p. 8.)

Endnote 048

(See Plato, Republic, Book VII.)

Endnote 049

"Wherefore, since it is our duty fully to enjoy the truth which lives unchangeably . . . the soul must be purified that it may have power to perceive that light, and to rest in it when it is perceived. And let us look upon this purification as a kind of journey or voyage to our native land. For it is not by change of place that we can come nearer to Him who is in every place, but by the cultivation of pure desires and virtuous habits." (Christian Doctrine, I, p. 13.)

Endnote 050

"And my whole hope is only in Thy exceeding great mercy. Give what Thou commandest, and command what Thou wilt. Thou imposest continency upon us, 'nevertheless, when I perceived,' saith one, 'that I could not otherwise obtain her except God gave her me; . . . that was a point of wisdom also to know whose gift she was.' For by continency are we bound up and brought into one, whence we were scattered abroad into many. For he loves Thee too little who loves aught with Thee, which he loves not for Thee, O Love, who ever burnest, and art never quenched! O Charity, my God, kindle me! Thou commandest continency; give what Thou commandest and command what Thou wilt." (Confessions, p. 265.)

Lord Byron has reserved for himself the distinction of admitting an envious pleasure in those confessions of Augustine in which he refers to sins of the flesh: "Augustine in his fine confessions makes the reader envy his transgressions." (Don Juan, I, 47.) It requires Byron's perversity to pick out the congenial alloy, leaving unnoticed its setting of pure gold, where blaze the jewels of passionate penitence and humility, love, and greatness of soul. Nothing can exceed the healthy-mindedness and holy-mindedness of this "hot-blooded man's" (Harnack) self accusations, unless it be their severity. Pressensé comparing Augustine's Confessions with those of Rousseau, characterizes the one as "a grand act of penitence and love," and the other as "a cry of triumph in the very midst of his sin, and robing his shame in a royal purple."

Paul Janet says, with exquisite accuracy, in the Introduction to his translation of the Confessions: "Saint Augustine was a true sinner; he had, therefore, no need of fanatical faith in order to appease exaggerated remorse; he was a genuine sceptic, and had not, therefore, to seek in a fictitious faith an inadequate remedy to unmeasured doubt: simple faith sufficed him, but a faith which seeks to understand: fides quaerens intellectum; he remains a philosopher in becoming a believer. With Saint Augustine, the passions are the infirmities of a superior soul, a soul tender and fiery, which from infancy is revealed by two remarkable characteristics: the ardor of imagination and the desire of superiority and glory.

"He goes to the play to weep as he wept, when a child, over the misfortunes of Dido. But the spectacle of human passions does not suffice, he wishes to experience them. 'To love and be loved seemed to me the grandest thing in life.' He knew all the pleasures, all the sorrows of forbidden passions, and, as he himself tells us, with an incomparable eloquence, 'in the very heart of pleasure, he was bound by the knots of anguish, and tortured by the burning irons of jealousy, by suspicions, by fears, by furies, by quarrels.' Nothing more sensitive, more alive, than this portrayal: perhaps it is even too true to life, perhaps in the charm and emotion of these too bold and too faithful portrayals, one overlooks the moment of repentance and expiation."

But it is Augustine himself who best explains, apologizes, comments. He says of his Confessions: "What then have I to do with men, that they should hear my confessions, as if they were going to cure all my diseases? . . . But yet do Thou, my most secret Physician, make clear to me what fruit I may reap by doing it. For the confessions of my past sins, — which Thou hast 'forgiven' and 'covered' that Thou mightest make me happy in Thee, changing my soul by faith, and Thy sacrament, — when they are read and heard, stir up the heart, that it sleep not in despair and say 'I cannot:' but that it may awake in the love of Thy mercy and the sweetness of Thy grace, by which he that is weak is strong, if by it he is made conscious of his own weakness. As for the good, they take delight in hearing of the past errors of such as are now freed from them; and they delight, not because they are errors, but because they have been, and are so no longer." (Confessions, pp. 239, 240.)

Endnote 051

"Augustine devoted voluntarily a part of the night to reviewing, in quiet and composure, the questions which had occupied the day. One may see in Chapter 3 of the book on Order, in the example of Augustine and his friends, what activity, what passion, the men of his time carried into their search after wisdom and truth, and how justified is the remark of Erasmus, that 'they were as eager for knowledge as a trader is to make money.' " (Soliloquies, Pelissier's translation, note 25.)

Endnote 052

"The prayer with which this work begins is of touching beauty; it evidently inspired the prayer which Fénelon placed at the conclusion of his treatise on the Existence of God." (Histoire de Saint Augustin, Poujoulat, p. 113.)

"The knowledge by which we know that we live is the most inward of all knowledge, of which even the Academic cannot insinuate" (Trinity, p. 402). "But, without any delusive representation of images or phantasms, I am most certain that I am, and that I know and delight in this. In respect of these truths, I am not at all afraid of the arguments of the Academicians, who say: 'What if you are deceived?' For if I am deceived, I am." (City of God, Vol. I, p. 468.)

"This is one of the passages cited by Sir William Hamilton, along with the Cogito, ergo sum of Descartes, in confirmation of his proof, that in so far as we are conscious of certain modes of existence, in so far we possess an absolute certainty that we exist." (Ibid. note.)

Endnote 054

"Yet who ever doubts that he himself lives, and remembers, and understands, and wills, and thinks, and knows, and judges? Seeing that even if he doubts, he lives: if he doubts, he remembers why he doubts: if he doubts, he understands that he doubts: if he doubts, he wishes to be certain: if he doubts, he thinks." (Trinity, Book X, p. 256.)

Endnote 055

"Here is the whole of the philosophy of Descartes. Subjective evidence considered as the foundation of certainty. Without desiring to despoil Descartes of his glory, we love to make it apparent that Saint Augustine is the father of the philosophic school of the seventeenth century, a school altogether French and Catholic, dethroned by Locke and Condillac, eloquently attacked twenty years ago in the name of the interests of the Christian faith, but destined, as we hope, to recapture the empire in our midst." (Poujoulat, Saint Augustin, p. 115.)

Poujoulat's hope, expressed over fifty years ago, is already realized according to Foster, who says of the philosophy of Kant and Descartes, without, however, giving Augustine the credit of being its father: "This is the imperishable merit and message of the Kantian epistemology — with Descartes the father of modern philosophy, as forerunner, since he proclaimed the thinking self, as the fixed point over against all doubt, and especially as the starting point for the construction of our world." (Finality of the Christian Religion, p. 225.) "For not only he who says, 'I know,' and says so truly, must needs know what knowing is; but he also who says, 'I do not know,' and says so confidently and truly, and knows that he says so truly, certainly knows what knowing is; for he both distinguishes him who does not know from him who knows, when he looks into himself, and says truly 'I do not know;' and whereas he knows that he says this truly, whence should he know it, if he did not know what knowing is?" (Trinity, X, p. 245.)

Endnote 056

"This entrance upon the second book completely conformed to the habits of sceptic and dialecticians, pursued by the fear of supplying arguments against themselves, recalls the systematic doubt of Descartes and the first pages of his Second Meditation. Only the doubt of St. Augustine is concerned here with problems, which are really proper subjects of discussion, while that of Descartes is applied to incontestable verities, like that of the existence of the body." (Pelissier's translation of Soliloquies, note 26.)

Endnote 057

"Erasmus calls attention with reason to this sophism concerning Truth, which is treated like an actual entity at one time, at another, like a true judgment. The manner in which Reason here plays with her interlocutor, recalls the malicious pleasure which Socrates often found in embarrassing his disciples or his adversaries. One suffers in seeing a pure and true doctrine compromised by such an admixture of wretched arguities." (Pelissier's translation of Soliloquies, note 27.)

Endnote 058

"As then we speak of bodies feeling and living, though the feeling and life of the body are from the soul, so also we speak of bodies being pained, though no pain can be suffered by the body apart from the soul." (City of God, XXI, p. 416.)

"Nor did I ever with perception of the body either see, hear, smell, taste or touch my joy; but I experienced it in my mind when I rejoiced." (Confessions, X, p. 259.)

Endnote 059

"The same sophism concerning the false, considered here in the character of certain judgments; there in that of false things; and again, as a sort of entity of which he strives to determine the existence. Erasmus has again called attention to this bad argumentation." (Soliloquies, Pelissier's translation, note 8.)

Endnote 060

"There is a tendency to call the argument or statement that, whatever faculty man possesses, the Deity must have also, by the term 'Anthropomorphism;' but it seems to me a misnomer, and to convey quite wrong ideas. The argument represented by 'He that formed the eye, shall he not see? He that planted the ear, shall he not hear?' need not assume for a moment that God has sense organs akin to those of man, or that He appreciates ethereal and aerial vibrations in the same sort of way." (Lodge, Life and Matter, p. 64.)

Endnote 061

If Augustine lived to-day, how would the theologians, philosophers, psychologists classify him? The answer to this question must depend, alas! on the parti pris of the individual. Monism in any guise except that of materialistic monism might claim him, for constantly he suggests pantheism, acosmism, even solipsism, either of which, in a last analysis, resolves itself into the All in All.

Dualism could claim him, for, after his conversion, he nowhere allows that man was of the same substance with God; and though man was created by God in His own image, he was no more than a candidate for immortality, and only could, by it, arrive at reality. Man actually exists only if he persists, for only that which abides has true being. His Dualism was therefore hypothetical. As Harnack says: "Everything which was not God, including his own soul . . . appeared as the absolutely transient, therefore as non-existent; for no true being exists, where there is also not-being; therefore God exists alone (God the only substance). On the other hand, as far as it possessed a relative existence, it seemed good, very good, as an evolution of the divine Being (the many as the embodiment, emanating and ever-returning, of the One)." Later his Dualism was less evanescent. His theory of creation, founded on a literal adoption of the statement in Genesis, introduced the "other" substance, "not nothing," "not almost nothing," but not God, yet, "created by His breath" (See note 4). Matter appears, and Dualism is alive forevermore in the thought and speech of men. Logic is king with a tyrant's power, to use it henceforth like a tyrant. Its sanest victims take their refuge to-day in the becoming watchword "Ignoramus," and if a venturesome one, under strong provocation, makes a protest, he does it in the subjunctive mood as does Sir Oliver Lodge: "There seems some reason to suppose that anything that actually exists, must be in some way or other perpetual . . . there may be in each a fundamental substratum which, if it can be reached, will be found to be eternal." (Life and Matter, p. 30.) Augustine affirmed his ignorance, but in "phrases slightly different from the parish priest" (Faust) or the modern Academician, for he affirmed his belief as well; and he made his hypotheses; but his beliefs and hypotheses never petrified into rigid dogmas in his own mind. Harnack says: "Where Augustine put the question of creation in the form 'How is the unity of being related to plurality of manifestation?' the notion of creation is really always eliminated But he never entirely gave up this way of putting the question, for, at bottom things possess their independence only in their manifestation, while in so far as they exist, they form the ground of knowledge for the existence of God. But besides this Augustine still asserted vigorously the creatio ex nihilo (omnes naturae ex deo, non de deo. De nat. bon. c. Manich. I)." (History of Dogma, V, p. 115, note 3.)

Yes, he did; and he may be right or wrong. But the reason, the sole reason, for this great man's theological, i. e. philosophical, inconsistency in this assertion, as well as his ethical inconsistency in his affirmations concerning predestination, arose from his wholesale acceptance of the most extreme doctrine of plenary inspiration; he was obliged to accept "Moses" (Confessions, p. 344 et seq.) and Paul as the speaking tubes for the "Eternal Truth" to the last word and punctuation of its verbal form.

Let no modern man, with his modern inconsistencies, throw the first stone! With Augustine it was "Let God be true but every man a liar." Authority construed "God" and "true" and pushed Reason to the rear. What agony this submission to conscience cost him, let only him who recants righteous reason in obedience to authority say! But oh, the pity of it! and oh, for an Augustine to stand with like loyalty to a less encumbered Truth in the forefront of to-day's battle!

Endnote 062

"Bossuet has reproduced this definition in his treatise on the knowledge of God and the self." (Saint Augustin, Poujoulat, p. 116.)

Endnote 063

"Alas for me, that I do not, at least, know the extent of my own ignorance! Behold, O my God, before Thee I lie not. As I speak so is my heart. Thou shalt light my candle: Thou, O Lord my God, wilt enlighten my darkness." (Confessions, Book II, chap. 25.)

Endnote 064

A little later Augustine wrote his six books upon music. Villemain says (Tableau de l'Éloquence, p. 421): "The duration of syllables, their value and their combinations, all the effects of rhythm, all the varieties of metre, all the forms of verse, are explained with a curious exactitude which resembles that of Quintilian in some chapters, or of a compatriot of Augustine's, Terentianus Maurus in his didactic poem. One is not surprised that this oratorical and poetic science of numbers, to which Cicero attaches so much importance in his essays upon eloquence, should have so greatly occupied the brilliant rhetorician. But that, after all, is only a part and the material part of the art. Six other books should have treated of melody, and would, undoubtedly, have comprised the moral views of Plato upon music and the poetry which Christian inspiration would have also added."

The faithful Poujoulat explains this deviation of the church father-to-be thus: "The six books upon Music composed in his hours of leisure, had for their aim to lead those who love letters and poetry to God, the eternal harmony. Augustine recognized the fact that music is one of the greatest agencies for arriving at the magnificent marvels of the Infinite. In his review (Retractations) of these works, the doctor treated his six books on music severely because he judged them from the point of view of the seriousness of his position as bishop; and pious authors have believed it their duty to agree in this severity. But it becomes a less exclusive appreciator to give to genius all the glory of its work, and to acquit it when it blames itself too scrupulously."

Endnote 065

"This absurd conclusion is a consequence of the confusion made by the interlocuteurs between the different applications of the words false and true. Augustine ought to have said that it is by the resemblance to others, that certain things deceive us as to their nature, and cause us to entertain false judgments; such is really the rôle of resemblance in this case." (Soliloquies, Pelissier's translation, p. 154.)

Augustine, always true to human nature, commends to all readers the unhappy truth of his observation: "The science of reasoning is of very great service in searching into and unravelling all sorts of questions that come up in Scripture, only in the use of it we must guard against the love of wrangling, and the childish vanity of entrapping an adversary." (Christian Doctrine, p. 68.)

This looks very much as if Augustine, in the land of crocodiles, evolved his idea of it from the bowels of his consciousness. The crocodile (see Cicero, Tusculum Disputations V: 27) was held sacred by the Egyptians, and, like some specially venerated and privileged species in the genus homo, developed, therefore, extraordinary powers!

"Everywhere, O Truth, dost Thou direct all who consult Thee, and dost at once answer all, though they consult Thee on divers things. Clearly dost Thou answer, though all do not with clearness hear. All consult Thee upon whatever they wish, though they hear not always that which they wish. He is Thy best servant who does not so much look to hear that from Thee which he himself wishes, as to wish that which he heareth from Thee." (Confessions, p. 263.)

Pelissier (Note 35, Soliloquies) appends a tabulated résumé of the foregoing reasoning which he calls "a long tissue of sophisms." We must own, with M. Saisset (Preface to translation of City of God), that some of Augustine's arguments are "more ingenious than solid" and, with Erasmus, that he indulges sometimes in "obscure subtility and unpleasant prolixity," although he adds "the toil of penetrating the apparent obscurities will be rewarded by finding a real wealth of insight and enlightment."

We have this testimony of Scipio recorded in Cicero: "They (the Romans) considered comedy and all theatrical performances as disgraceful, and therefore not only debarred players from offices and honors open to ordinary citizens, but also decreed that their names should be branded by the censor, and erased from the roll of their tribe." (City of God, Book II, p. 62.)

"Again, the science of definition, of division, of partition, although it is frequently applied to falsities, is not itself false, nor framed by man's device, but is evolved from the reason of things. For although poets have applied it to their fictions, and false philosophers or even heretics — that is, false Christians — to their erroneous doctrines, that is no reason why it should be false, for example, that neither in definition, nor in division, nor in partition, is anything to be included that does not pertain to the matter in hand, nor anything to be omitted that does. This is true, even though the things to be defined or divided are not true. The definition and division, therefore, of what is false may be perfectly true, although what is false cannot, of course, itself be true." (Christian Doctrine, pp. 70, 71.)

"After that I was put to school to get learning of which I (worthless as I was) knew not what use there was; and yet, if slow to learn, I was flogged! for this was deemed praiseworthy by our forefathers, and many before us, passing the same course, had appointed beforehand for us these troublesome ways by which we were compelled to pass, multiplying labour and sorrow upon the sons of Adam. But we found, O Lord, men praying to Thee, and we learned from them to conceive of Thee, according to our ability, to be some Great One, who was able (though not visible to our senses) to hear and help us.

"For as a boy I began to pray to Thee my 'help' and my 'refuge,' and in invoking Thee, broke the bands of my tongue, and entreated Thee, though little, with no little earnestness, that I might not be beaten at school. And when Thou heardest me not, giving me not over to folly thereby, my elders, yea, and my own parents too, who wished me no ill, laughed at my stripes, my then great and grievous ill." (Confessions, Book I, p. 11.)

Endnote 073

In all this worrying of the reader over "the science of disputation," we, of the modern mind and method, must remember that to those of Augustine's day, this worrying was, as it had been for centuries, the sine qua non of intellectual life. No one, in that day of the world, dreamed of excavating "Truth" after the modern Teutonic's method, in the solitude of an attic with no companions save his beer-mug and his pipe. Men talked it over; they had words with each other; to the victor belonged the spoils, and it was 'devil take the hind-most.' It was the method of Socrates, Plato, and Aristotle, and revered, as these masters were revered. Socrates declared that the most excellent men, the happiest and the most eloquent, were formed by this art. Augustine says: "I studied books of eloquence, wherein I was eager to be eminent, from a damnable and inflated purpose, even a delight in human vanity;" . . . and he says that Ambrose, to whom his mother appealed in his behalf, told her that he had already perplexed divers inexperienced persons with vexatious questions. In an interesting passage in his work against Manichæism, he tells us that his victories over "inexperienced persons" stimulated him to fresh conquests, and thus kept him bound longer than he would otherwise have been in the chains of this heresy. (Confessions, p. 55, note.)

But he had a conscience even then about the use he made of his dialectical skill. "In those years I taught the art of rhetoric and, overcome by cupidity, put to sale a loquacity by which to overcome. Yet I preferred, Lord, Thou knowest, to have honest scholars (as they are esteemd); and these I, without artifice, taught artifices, not to be put in practice against the life of the guiltless, though sometimes for the life of the guilty." (Confessions, Book IV, p. 57.)

This conscience asserted itself more and more. In the first book, itself the product of discussion with his friends, written from Cassiacum, he says: "When one disputes, the great matter is, not to have made great progress in wisdom, but to be moved only by the desire of attaining truth and reason, and to feel only contempt for victory." (Against the Academician, Book I, chap. 9.)

And when his long life of controversy was nearly ended, he writes: "The art of disputation previously spoken of, which deals with inferences, and definitions, and divisions, is of the greatest assistance in the discovery of the meaning, provided only that men do not fall into the error of supposing that when they have learnt these things they have learnt the true secret of a happy life. . . . And in regard to all these laws, we derive more pleasure from them as exhibitions of truth, than assistance in arguing or forming opinions, except perhaps that they put the intellect in better training. We must take care, however, that they do not at the same time make it more inclined to mischief or vanity, that is to say, that they do not give those who have learnt them an inclination to lead people astray by plausible speech and catching questions, or make them think that they have attained some great thing that gives them an advantage over the good and innocent." (Christian Doctrine, Book II, pp. 72, 73.)

Endnote 074

Augustine here suggests his familiarity with Aristotle, the acquisition of which he thus describes: "And what did it profit me that when scarce twenty years old, a book of Aristotle's, entitled The Ten Predicaments, fell into my hands, — on whose very name I hung as on something great and divine, when my rhetoric master of Carthage and others who were esteemed learned, referred to it with cheeks swelling with pride, — I read it alone and understood it? . . . And the book appeared to me to speak plainly enough of substances, such as man is, and of their qualities, such as the figure of a man, of what kind it is; and his stature, how many feet high; and his relationship, whose brother he is, or where placed, or when born, or whether he stands or sits, or is shod or armed, or does or suffers any thing; and whatever innumerable things might be classed under these nine categories, — of which I have given some examples, — or under that chief category of substance. What did all this profit me, seeing it even hindered me, when, imagining that whatsoever existed was comprehended in those ten categories, I tried so to understand, O my God, Thy wonderful and unchangeable Unity, as if Thou also hadst been subjected to Thine own greatness or beauty, so that they should exist in Thee as their subject, like as in bodies, whereas Thou, Thyself, art Thy greatness and beauty." (Confessions, Book IV, pp. 78, 79.)

But he found later the more excellent way. Harnack says: "He became, because he was the counterpart of Aristotle, the true Aristotle of a new science, which seems indeed to have forgotten that as a theory of perception, and as inner observation, it originated in the monotheistic faith and life of prayer." We must add a few sentences from a parallel between Augustine and Aristotle by Siebeck, which Harnack quotes in full: "Questions of ethics which Aristotle handles from the standpoint of the relation of man to man, appear in Augustine in the light of the relations between his own heart and that of this known and felt God."

"Aristotle knows the wants of the inner life only so far as they are capable of developing the life, supported by energetic effort and philosophic equanimity, in and with society. He seems to hold that clear thinking and restfully energetic activity prevent all suffering and misfortune to society or the individual. The deeper sources of dispeace, of pain of soul, of unfulfilled wants of the heart, remain dark in his investigation. Augustine's significance begins just where the problem is to trace the unrest of the believing or seeking soul to its roots, and to make sure of the inner facts in which the heart can reach its rest. Even the old problems which he reviews and examines in their whole extent and meaning from the standpoint of his rich scientific culture, now appear in a new light. Therefore he can grasp, and at the same time deepen, everything which has come to him from Hellenism." . . .

"Aristotle, the Greek, was only interested in the life of the soul, in so far as it turned outward and helped to fathom the world theoretically and practically; Augustine, the first modern man . . . only took it into consideration, in so far as reflection upon it enabled him to conceive the inner character of personal life as something really independent of the outer world." Harnack adds: "It was possible to travel back along the line which had been traced by a millennium down to Augustine, and the positive capital which Neoplatonism and Augustine had received from the past, and had changed into negative values, could also be re-established with a positive force. But something had undoubtedly been lost: we find it surviving in almost none but those who were ignorant of theology and philosophy; we do not find it among thinkers; and that is frank joy in the phenomenal world, in its obvious meaning, and in calm and energetic work. If it were possible to unite in science and in the disposition, the piety, spirituality, and introspection of Augustine, with the openness to the world, the restful and energetic activity, and unclouded cheerfulness of antiquity, we should have reached the highest level." (History of Dogma, chap. IV, pp. 108, et seq.)

Endnote 075

Augustine has, perhaps, in mind here sentiments from the lost Hortensius, which he quotes many years later in his work on the Trinity with criticism matured in the interval. He says: "This contemplative wisdom, I say, it is that Cicero commends in the end of the dialogue Hortensius, when he says: 'While, then, we consider these things night and day, and sharpen our understanding, which is the eye of the mind, taking care that it be not ever dulled, that is, while we live in philosophy: we, I say, in so doing, have great hope that if, on the one hand, this sentiment and wisdom of ours is mortal and perishable, we shall still, when we have discharged our human offices, have a pleasant setting, and a not painful extinction, and as it were a rest from life: or of, on the other, as ancient philosophers thought — and those, too, the greatest and far the most celebrated — we have souls eternal and divine, then must we needs think, that the more these shall have always kept in their own proper course, i. e. in reason and in the desire of inquiry, and the less they shall have mixed and entangled themselves in the vices and errors of men, the more easy ascent and return they will have to heaven.' And then he says, adding this short sentence, and finishing his discourse by repeating it: 'Wherefore, to end my discourse at last, if we wish either for a tranquil extinction after living in the pursuit of these subjects, or if to migrate without delay from this present home to another in no little measure better, we must bestow all our labour and care upon these pursuits.' And here I marvel, that a man of such great ability should promise to men living in philosophy, which makes man blessed by contemplation of truth, 'A pleasant setting after the discharge of human offices, if this our sentiment and wisdom is mortal and perishable,' as if that which we did not love, or rather which we fiercely hated, were then to die and come to nothing, so that its setting would be pleasant to us. But indeed he had not learned this from the philosophers, whom he extols with great praise; but this sentiment is redolent of that New Academy, wherein it pleased him to doubt of even the plainest things. But from the philosophers that were greatest and far most celebrated, as he himself confesses, he had learned that souls are eternal. For souls that are eternal are not unsuitably stirred up by the exhortation to be found in 'their own proper course' when the end of this life shall have come, i. e., 'in reason and in the desire of inquiry,' and to mix and entangle themselves the less in the vices and errors of men, in order that they may have an easier return to God." (Trinity, Book IV, pp. 375, 376.)

Endnote 076

Two years later Augustine writes to Nebridius: "To occupy one's thoughts throughout life with journeyings which you cannot perform tranquilly and easily, is not the part of a man whose thoughts are engaged with that last journey which is called death, and which alone, as you understand, really deserves serious consideration. God has indeed granted to some few men whom He has ordained to bear rule over churches, the capacity of not only awaiting calmly, but even desiring eagerly, that last journey, while at the same time they can meet without disquietude the toils of those other journeyings: . . . Believe me there is need of much withdrawal of oneself from the tumult of the things which are passing away, in order that there may be formed in man, not through insensibility, not through presumption, not through vain glory, not through superstitious blindness, the ability to say 'I fear nought.' " (Letters, pp. 23, 24.)

Endnote 077

"Ambrose was sovereign among Western bishops, and at the same time the Greek trained exegete and theologian. In both qualities he acted on Augustine, who looked up to him as Luther did to Staupitz." It was "in Ambrose, the priestly Chancellor of the state, that the imperial power (imperium) of the Catholic church dawned upon him, and his experiences of the confusion and weakness of the civil power at the beginning of the fifth century completed the impression. Along with this Ambrose's sermons fall to be considered. If on one side, they were wholly dependent on Greek models, yet they show, on the other hand, in their practical tone, the spirit of the West. Augustine's demand that the preacher should 'teach, sway, and move' (docere, flectere, movere) is as if drawn from those sermons." (History of Dogma, V, pp. 30, 48.)

Endnote 078

"Nor did I now groan in my prayers that Thou would'st help me; but my mind was wholly intent on knowledge, and eager to dispute. And Ambrose himself I esteemed a happy man, as the world counted happiness, in that such great personages held him in honour; only his celibacy appeared to me a painful thing. But what hope he cherished, what struggles he had against the temptations that beset his very excellences, what solace in adversities, and what savoury joys Thy bread possessed for the hidden mouth of his heart when ruminating on it, I could neither conjecture nor had I experienced. Nor did he know my embarrassments, nor the pit of my danger. For I could not request of him what I wished as I wished, in that I was debarred from hearing and speaking to him by crowds of busy people, whose infirmities he devoted himself to. With whom when he was not engaged (which was but a little time) he either was refreshing his body with necessary sustenance, or his mind with reading. But while reading, his eyes glanced over the pages, and his heart searched out the sense, but his voice and tongue were silent. Ofttimes, when we had come (for no one was forbidden to enter, nor was it his custom that the arrival of those who came should be announced to him), we saw him thus reading to himself, and never otherwise; and having long sat in silence (for who durst interrupt one so intent?) we were fain to depart, inferring that in the little time he secured for the recruiting of his mind, free from the clamour of other men's business, he was unwilling to be taken off. . . . But whatever was his motive in so doing, doubtless, in such a man, was a good one. But verily no opportunity could I find of ascertaining what I desired from that Thy so holy oracle, his breast, unless the thing might be entered into briefly. But those surgings in me required to find him at full leisure, that I might pour them out to him, but never were they able to find him so." (Confessions, pp. 112, 113.)

Endnote 079

"Zenobius, man of letters and poet, who, without doubt, belonged or inclined to the new faith by philosophic contemplation. More than once Zenobius had asked concerning the question of Providence, and in hurried interviews and by verse, — 'and by good verse, too' — says Augustine. While exposing his own views and doubts, he had besought a response." (Tableau de l'Éloquence, p. 394.)

Endnote 080

"Tu enim si deseris, peritur; sed non deseris, quia tu es summum bonum, quod nemo recte quaesivit et minime invenit." (Soliloquies, I, 6.)

Endnote 081

"For verses and poems I can turn into true food, but the 'Medea flying' though I sang, I maintained it not; though I heard it sung, I believed it not." (Confessions, p. 45.)

Endnote 082

"This expression 'incapable of witness-bearing' signified both ineligibility as a witness and also as assisting at the making of a will." (Pelissier's translation of Soliloquies, note 44.)

Endnote 083

"I perceive that all those images which you as well as many others call phantasiae, may be most conveniently and accurately divided into three classes, according as they originate with the senses, or the imagination, or the faculty of reason.

"Examples of the first class are when my mind forms within itself and presents to me the image of your face, or of Carthage, or of our departed friend Verecundus, or of any other thing at present or formerly existing, which I have myself seen and perceived.

"Under the second class come all things which we imagine to have been, or to be so and so: e. g. when for the sake of illustration in discourse, we ourselves suppose things which have no existence, but which are not prejudicial to truth: or when we call up to our own minds a lively conception of the things described while we read history, or hear, or compose, or refuse to believe fabulous narrations. Thus, according to my own fancy, and as it may occur to my own mind, I picture to myself the appearance of Æneas, or of Medea with her team of winged dragons, or of Chremes or Parmeno. . . . As for the third class of images, it has to do chiefly with numbers and measures; which are found partly in the nature of things, as when the figure of the entire world is discovered and an image consequent upon this discovery is formed in the mind of one thinking upon it; and partly in sciences, as in geometrical figures and musical harmonies, and in the infinite variety of numerals; which, although they are, as I think, true in themselves as objects of the understanding, are nevertheless the causes of illusive exercises of the imagination, the misleading tendency of which reason itself can only with difficulty withstand; although it is not easy to preserve even the science of reasoning free from this evil, since in our logical divisions and conclusions we form to ourselves, so to speak, calculi or counters to facilitate the process of reasoning." (Letters, I, p. 15, et seq.)

Endnote 084

This is, of course, Plato's doctrine of reminiscence, as we find it in the Phaedo and elsewhere. Augustine thought differently later. He says in his Retractations, referring to this passage: "I recant this doctrine. It is more credible that ignorant persons make correct replies to questions which are put to them because they have in them, as much as they are capable of having, the light of eternal reason, where they see these unchangeable verities. It is not that they have once known and have forgotten them, according to that opinion of Plato and his disciples. I have refuted this opinion as far as my subject furnished me an occasion, in Book XII of the treatise concerning the Trinity, Chapter 15."

He refers to this passage: "And hence that noble philosopher, Plato, endeavored to persuade us that the souls of men lived here, even before they bare these bodies; and that hence those things which are learnt, are rather remembered as having been known already, than taken into knowledge as things new. For he has told us that a boy, when questioned I know not what respecting geometry, replied as if he were perfectly skilled in that branch of learning. For being questioned step by step, and skillfully, he saw what was to be seen, and said that which he saw. But if this had been a recollecting of things previously known, then certainly every one, or almost every one, would not have been able so to answer when questioned. For not every one was a geometrician in the former life, since geometricians are so few among men that scarcely one can be found anywhere. But we ought rather to believe that the intellectual mind is so formed in its nature as to see those things, which by the disposition of the Creator are subjoined to things intelligible in a natural order, by a sort of incorporeal light of an unique kind; as the eye of the flesh sees things adjacent to itself in this bodily light, of which light, it is made to be receptive and adapted to it." (Trinity, Book XII, p. 304.)

"Again, when I call back to my mind some arch turned beautifully and symmetrically, which, let us say, I saw at Carthage; a certain reality that had been made known to the mind through the eyes, and transferred to the memory, causes the imaginary view. But I behold in my mind yet another thing, according to which that work of art pleases me, and whence also, if it displeases me, I should correct it. We judge therefore of those particular things according to that (form of eternal truth), and discern that form by the intuition of the rational mind. But those things themselves we either touch if present by the bodily sense, or if absent remember their images as fixed in our memory, or picture, in the way of likeness to them, such things as we ourselves also, if we wished and were able, would laboriously build up; figuring in the mind after one fashion the images of bodies, or seeing bodies through the body; but after another, grasping by simple intelligence what is above the eye of the mind, viz.: the reasons and the unspeakably beautiful skill of such forms. We behold then by the sight of the mind, in that eternal truth from which all things temporal are made, the form according to which we are, and according to which we do anything by true and right reason, either in ourselves, or in things corporeal; and we have the true knowledge of things, thence conceived, as it were as a word within us, and by speaking we beget it from within; nor by being born does it depart from us." (Trinity, Book IX, p. 233.)

Endnote 085

Pelissier says of this:

"The distinction is delicate and exact. It is necessary to distinguish, among the operations of the intellect, apart from the poetic and creative imagination, the faculty of representing objects under images and the conceptional faculty, which operates as abstract thought and has no help from the material world. Less seductive and less fêted, this latter faculty is rarer and more elevated in the order of intellectual things." He also adds a fine passage from M. Cournot and refers the reader to Descartes' Meditation Cinquième (Soliloquies, Pelissier's translation, note 50.)

Endnote 086

"But if the soul die, what then?" "Why then truth dies, or intelligence is not truth, or intelligence is not a part of the soul, or that which has some part immortal is liable to die; conclusions all of which I demonstrated long ago in my Soliloquies to be absurd because impossible; and I am firmly persuaded that this is the case, but somehow through the influence of custom in the experience of evils we are terrified, and hesitate." (Letters, I, p. 8.)

www.ingramcontent.com/pod-product-compliance
Lightning Source LLC
Chambersburg PA
CBHW081240020426
42331CB00013B/3234